Bloom's BioCritiques

Dante Alighieri
Maya Angelou
Jane Austen
James Baldwin
William Blake
Jorge Luis Borges
The Brontë Sisters
Lord Byron
Geoffrey Chaucer
Anton Chekhov
Joseph Conrad
Stephen Crane
Charles Dickens
Emily Dickinson
William Faulkner
F. Scott Fitzgerald
Robert Frost
Ernest Hemingway
Langston Hughes
Zora Neale Hurston
Franz Kafka
Stephen King
Gabriel García Márquez
Herman Melville
Arthur Miller
John Milton
Toni Morrison
Edgar Allan Poe
J.D. Salinger
William Shakespeare
John Steinbeck
Henry David Thoreau
Mark Twain
Alice Walker
Eudora Welty
Walt Whitman
Tennessee Williams

Bloom's BioCritiques

JAMES BALDWIN

Edited and with an introduction by
Harold Bloom
Sterling Professor of the Humanities
Yale University

CHELSEA HOUSE
PUBLISHERS
A Haights Cross Communications ✦ Company®
Philadelphia

Library of Congress Cataloging-in-Publication Data

James Baldwin / [edited by] Harold Bloom.
    p. cm. — (Bloom's biocritiques)
  Includes bibliographical references and index.
  ISBN 0-7910-8575-9
  1. Baldwin, James, 1924——-Criticism and interpretation. 2. African Americans
in literature. I. Bloom, Harold. II. Series.
  PS3552.A45Z723 2005
  818'.5409—dc22
                                        2005011380

Contributing editor: Gabriel Welsch
Cover design by Keith Trego
Cover: © Bettman/CORBIS
Layout by EJB Publishing Services

CONTENTS

User's Guide

These volumes are designed to introduce the reader to the life and work of the world's literary masters. Each volume begins with Harold Bloom's essay "The Work in the Writer" and a volume-specific introduction also written by Professor Bloom. Following these unique introductions is an engaging biography that discusses the major life events and important literary accomplishments of the author under consideration.

Furthermore, each volume includes an original critique that not only traces the themes, symbols, and ideas apparent in the author's works, but strives to put those works into a cultural and historical perspective. In addition to the original critique is a brief selection of significant critical essays previously published on the author and his or her works followed by a concise and informative chronology of the writer's life. Finally, each volume concludes with a bibliography of the writer's works, a list of additional readings, and an index of important themes and ideas.

HAROLD BLOOM

The Work in the Writer

Literary biography found its masterpiece in James Boswell's *Life of Samuel Johnson*. Boswell, when he treated Johnson's writings, implicitly commented upon Johnson as found in his work, even as in the great critic's life. Modern instances of literary biography, such as Richard Ellmann's lives of W.B. Yeats, James Joyce, and Oscar Wilde, essentially follow in Boswell's pattern.

That the writer somehow is in the work, we need not doubt, though with William Shakespeare, writer-of-writers, we almost always need to rely upon pure surmise. The exquisite rancidities of the Problem Plays or Dark Comedies seem to express an extraordinary estrangement of Shakespeare from himself. When we read or attend *Troilus and Cressida* and *Measure for Measure*, we may be startled by particular speeches of Ulysses in the first play, or of Vincentio in the second. These speeches, of Ulysses upon hierarchy or upon time, or of Duke Vincentio upon death, are too strong either for their contexts or for the characters of their speakers. The same phenomenon occurs with Parolles, the military impostor of *All's Well That Ends Well*. Utterly disgraced, he nevertheless affirms: "Simply the thing I am / Shall make me live."

In Shakespeare, more even than in his peers, Dante and Cervantes, meaning always starts itself again through excess or overflow. The strongest of Shakespeare's creatures—Falstaff, Hamlet, Iago, Lear, Cleopatra—have an exuberance that is fiercer than their plays can contain. If Ben Jonson was at all correct in his complaint that "Shakespeare wanted art," it could have been only in a sense that he may not have intended. Where do the personalities of Falstaff or Hamlet touch a limit? What was it in Shakespeare that made *Hamlet* and the two parts of *Henry IV* into "plays unlimited"? Neither Falstaff nor Hamlet will be stopped: their wit, their beautiful, laughing speech, their intensity of being—all these are virtually infinite.

In what ways do Falstaff and Hamlet manifest the writer in the work? Evidently, we can never know, or know enough to answer with any authority. But what would happen if we reversed the question, and asked: How did the work form the writer, Shakespeare?

Of Shakespeare's inwardness, his biography tells us nothing. And yet, to an astonishing extent, Shakespeare created our inwardness. At the least, we can speculate that Shakespeare so lived his life as to conceal the depths of his nature, particularly as he rather prematurely aged. We do not have Shakespeare on Shakespeare, as any good reader of the Sonnets comes to realize: they do not constitute a key that unlocks his heart. No sequence of sonnets could be less confessional or more powerfully detached from the poet's self.

The German poet and universal genius, Goethe, affords a superb contrast to Shakespeare. Of Goethe's life, we know more than everything; I wonder sometimes if we know as much about Napoleon or Freud or any other human being who ever has lived, as we know about Goethe. Everywhere, we can find Goethe in his work, so much so that Goethe seems to crowd the writing out, just as Byron and Oscar Wilde seem to usurp their own literary accomplishments. Goethe, cunning beyond measure, nevertheless invested a rival exuberance in his greatest works that could match his personal charisma. The sublime out-rageousness of the Second Part of *Faust*, or of the greater lyric and meditative poems, forms a Counter-Sublime to Goethe's own daemonic intensity.

Goethe was fascinated by the daemonic in himself; we can doubt that Shakespeare had any such interests. Evidently, Shakespeare abandoned his acting career just before he composed *Measure for Measure* and *Othello*. I surmise that the egregious interventions by Vincentio and Iago displace the actor's energies into a new kind of mischief-making, a fresh opening to a subtler playwriting-within-the-play.

But what had opened Shakespeare to this new awareness? The answer is the work in the writer, *Hamlet* in Shakespeare. One can go further: it was not so much the play, *Hamlet*, as the character Hamlet, who changed Shakespeare's art forever.

Hamlet's personality is so large and varied that it rivals Goethe's own. Ironically Goethe's Faust, his Hamlet, has no personality at all, and is as colorless as Shakespeare himself seems to have chosen to be. Yet nothing could be more colorful than the Second Part of *Faust*, which is peopled by an astonishing array of monsters, grotesque devils and classical ghosts.

A contrast between Shakespeare and Goethe demonstrates that in each—but in very different ways—we can better find the work in the person, than we can discover that banal entity, the person in the work. Goethe to many of his contemporaries seemed to be a mortal god. Shakespeare, so far as we know, seemed an affable, rather ordinary fellow, who aged early and became somewhat withdrawn. Yet Faust, though Mephistopheles battles for his soul, is hardly worth the trouble unless you take him as an idea and not as a person. Hamlet is nearly every-idea-in-one, but he is precisely a personality and a person.

Would Hamlet be so astonishingly persuasive if his father's ghost did not haunt him? Falstaff is more alive than Prince Hal, who says that the devil haunts him in the shape of an old fat man. Three years before composing the final *Hamlet*, Shakespeare invented Falstaff, who then never ceased to haunt his creator. Falstaff and Hamlet may be said to best represent the work in the writer, because their influence upon Shakespeare was prodigious. W.H. Auden accurately observed that Falstaff possesses infinite energy: never tired, never bored, and absolutely both witty and happy until Hal's rejection destroys him. Hamlet too has infinite energy, but in him it is more curse than blessing.

Falstaff and Hamlet can be said to occupy the roles in Shakespeare's invented world that Sancho Panza and Don Quixote possess in Cervantes's. Shakespeare's plays from 1610 on (starting with *Twelfth Night*) are thus analogous to the Second Part of Cervantes's epic novel. Sancho and the Don overtly jostle Cervantes for authorship in the Second Part, even as Cervantes battles against the impostor who has pirated a continuation of his work. As a dramatist, Shakespeare manifests the work in the writer more indirectly. Falstaff's prose genius is revived in the scapegoating of Malvolio by Maria and Sir Toby Belch, while Falstaff's darker insights are developed by Feste's melancholic wit. Hamlet's intellectual resourcefulness, already deadly, becomes poisonous in Iago and in Edmund. Yet we have not crossed into the deeper abysses of the work in the writer in later Shakespeare.

No fictive character, before or since, is Falstaff's equal in self-trust. Sir John, whose delight in himself is contagious, has total confidence both in his self-awareness and in the resources of his language. Hamlet, whose self is as strong, and whose language is as copious, nevertheless distrusts both the self and language. Later Shakespeare is, as it were, much under the influence both of Falstaff and of Hamlet, but they tug him in opposite directions. Shakespeare's own copiousness of language is well-nigh incredible: a vocabulary in excess of twenty-one thousand words, almost eighteen hundred of which he coined himself. And of his word-hoard, nearly half are used only once each, as though the perfect setting for each had been found, and need not be repeated. Love for language and faith in language are Falstaffian attributes. Hamlet will darken both that love and that faith in Shakespeare, and perhaps the Sonnets can best be read as Falstaff and Hamlet counterpointing against one another.

Can we surmise how aware Shakespeare was of Falstaff and Hamlet, once they had played themselves into existence? *Henry IV, Part I* appeared in six quarto editions during Shakespeare's lifetime; *Hamlet* possibly had four. Falstaff and Hamlet were played again and again at the Globe, but Shakespeare knew also that they were being read, and he must have had contact with some of those readers. What would it have been like to discuss Falstaff or Hamlet with one of their early readers (presumably also part of their audience at the Globe), if you were the creator of such demiurges? The question would seem nonsensical to most Shakespeare scholars, but then these days they tend to be either ideologues or moldy figs. How can we recover the uncanniness of Falstaff and of Hamlet, when they now have become so familiar?

A writer's influence upon himself is an unexplored problem in criticism, but such an influence is never free from anxieties. The biocritical problem (which this series attempts to explore) can be divided into two areas, difficult to disengage fully. Accomplished works affect the author's life, and also affect her subsequent writings. It is simpler for me to surmise the effect of *Mrs. Dalloway* and *To the Lighthouse* upon Woolf's late *Between the Acts*, than it is to relate Clarissa Dalloway's suicide and Lily Briscoe's capable endurance in art to the tragic death and complex life of Virginia Woolf.

There are writers whose lives were so vivid that they seem sometimes to obscure the literary achievement: Byron, Wilde, Malraux, Hemingway. But most major Western writers do not live that exuberantly, and the greatest of all, Shakespeare, sometimes appears to have adopted the personal mask of colorlessness. And yet there are heroes of literature who struggled titanically with their own eras— Tolstoy, Milton, Victor Hugo—who nevertheless matter more for their works than their lives.

There are great figures—Emily Dickinson, Wallace Stevens, Willa Cather—who seem to have had so little of the full intensity of life when compared to the vitality of their work, that we might almost speak of the work in the work, rather than even of the work in a person. Emily Brontë might well be the extreme instance of such a visionary, surpassing William Blake in that one regard.

I conclude this general introduction to a series of literary bio-critiques by stating a tentative formula or principle for gauging the many ways in which the work influences the person and her subsequent, later work. Our influence upon ourselves is always related to the Shakespearean invention of self-overhearing, which I have written about in several other contexts. Life, as well as poetry and prose, is overheard rather than simply heard. The writer listens to herself as though she were somebody else, and the will to change begins to operate. The forces that live in us include the prior work we have done, and the dreams and waking visions that evade our dismissals.

HAROLD BLOOM

Introduction

I

Whatever the ultimate canonical judgment upon James Baldwin's fiction may prove to be, his nonfictional work clearly has permanent status in American literature. Baldwin, a considerable moral essayist, is comparable to George Orwell as a prose Protestant in stance. The evangelical heritage never has abandoned the author of *Go Tell It on the Mountain*, and Baldwin, like so many American essayists since Emerson, possesses the fervor of a preacher. Unlike Emerson, Baldwin lacks the luxury of detachment, since he speaks, not for a displaced Yankee majority, but for a sexual minority within a racial minority, indeed for an aesthetic minority among black homosexuals.

Ultimately, Baldwin's dilemma as a writer compelled to address social torments and injustices is that he is a minority of one, a solitary voice breaking forth against himself (and all others) from within himself. Like Carlyle (and a single aspect of the perspectivizing Nietzsche), Baldwin is of the authentic lineage of Jeremiah, most inward of prophets. What Baldwin opposes is what might be called, in Jeremiah's language, the injustice of outwardness, which means that Baldwin always must protest, even in the rather unlikely event that his country ever were to turn from selfishness and cruelty to justice and compassion in confronting its underclass of the exploited poor, whether blacks, Hispanics, or others cast out by the Reagan Revolution.

It seems accurate to observe that we remember Jeremiah, unlike

Amos or Micah, for his individuation of his own suffering, rather than for his social vision, such as it was. Baldwin might prefer to have been an Amos or a Micah, forerunners of Isaiah, rather than a Jeremiah, but like Jeremiah he is vivid as a rhetorician of his own psychic anguish and perplexities, and most memorable as a visionary of a certain involuntary isolation, an election that requires a dreadful cost of confirmation. As Baldwin puts it, the price of the ticket is to accept the real reasons for the human journey:

> The price the white American paid for his ticket was to become white—: and, in the main, nothing more than that, or, as he was to insist, nothing less. This incredibly limited not to say dimwitted ambition has choked many a human being to death here: and this, I contend, is because the white American has never accepted the real reasons for his journey. I know very well that my ancestors had no desire to come to this place: but neither did the ancestors of the people who became white and who require of my captivity a song. They require of me a song less to celebrate my captivity than to justify their own.

The Biblical text that Baldwin alludes to here, Psalm 137, does begin with the song of the exiles from Zion ("and they that wasted us required of us mirth") but ends with a ferocious prophecy against the wasters, ourselves. No writer—black or white—warns us so urgently of "the fire next time" as Baldwin and Jeremiah do, but I hear always in both prophets the terrible pathos of origins:

> Then the word of the Lord came unto me, saying,
> Before I formed thee in the belly I knew thee; and before thou camest forth out of the womb I sanctified thee, and I ordained thee a prophet unto the nations.
> Then said I, Ah, Lord God! behold, I cannot speak: for I am a child.

We: my family, the living and the dead, and the children coming along behind us. This was a complex matter, for I was not living with my family in Harlem, after all, but "down-town," in the "white world," in alien and mainly hostile territory. On the other hand, for me, then, Harlem was almost as alien and in a yet more intimidating way and risked being equally hostile, although for very different reasons. This truth cost me something in guilt and confusion, but it was the truth. It had something to do with my being the son of an evangelist and having been a child evangelist, but this is not all there was to it—that is, guilt is not all there was to it.

The fact that this particular child had been born when and where he was born had dictated certain expectations. The child does not really know what these expectations are—does not know how real they are—until he begins to fail, challenge, or defeat them. When it was clear, for example, that the pulpit, where I had made so promising a beginning, would not be my career, it was hoped that I would go on to college. This was never a very realistic hope and—perhaps because I knew this—I don't seem to have felt very strongly about it. In any case, this hope was dashed by the death of my father.

Once I had left the pulpit, I had abandoned or betrayed my role in the community—indeed, my departure from the pulpit and my leaving home were almost simultaneous. (I had abandoned the ministry in order not to betray myself by betraying the ministry.)

Reluctant prophets are in the position of Jonah; they provide texts for the Day of Atonement. Baldwin is always at work reexamining everything, doing his first works over; as he says: "Sing or shout or testify or keep it to yourself: but *know whence you came.*" We came crying hither because we came to this great stage of fools, but Baldwin, like Jeremiah and unlike Shakespeare, demands a theology of origins. He finds it in self-hatred, which he rightly insists is universal, though he seems to reject or just not be interested in the Freudian account of our moral masochism, our need for punishment. The evangelical sense of conscious sin remains strong in Baldwin. Yet, as a moral essayist, he is post-Christian, and persuades us that his prophetic stance is not so much religious as aesthetic. A kind of aesthetic of the moral life governs his vision, even in the turbulence of *The Fire Next Time* and *No Name in the Street*, and helps make them his finest achievements so far.

II

The center of Baldwin's prophecy can be located in one long, powerful paragraph of *The Fire Next Time*:

"The white man's Heaven," sings a Black Muslim minister, "is the black man's Hell." One may object—possibly—that this puts the matter somewhat too simply, but the song is true, and it has been true for as long as white men have ruled the world. The Africans put it another way: When the white man came to Africa, the white man had the Bible and the African had the land, but now it is the white man who is being, reluctantly and bloodily, separated from the land, and the African who is still attempting to digest or to vomit up the Bible. The struggle, therefore, that now begins in the world is extremely complex, involving the historical role of Christianity in the realm of power—that is, politics—and in the realm of morals. In the realm of power, Christianity has operated with an unmitigated arrogance and cruelty—necessarily, since a religion ordinarily imposes on those who have discovered the true faith, the spiritual duty of liberating the infidels. This particular true faith, moreover, is more deeply concerned about the soul than it is about the body, to which fact the flesh (and the corpses) of countless infidels bears witness. It goes without saying, then, that whoever questions the authority of the true faith also contests the right of the nations that hold this faith to rule over him—contests, in short, their title to his land. The spreading of the Gospel, regardless of the motives or the integrity or the heroism of some of the missionaries, was an absolutely indispensable justification for the planting of the flag. Priests and nuns and schoolteachers helped to protect and sanctify the power that was so ruthlessly being used by people who were indeed seeking a city, but not one in the heavens, and one to be made, very definitely, by captive hands. The Christian church itself—again, as distinguished from some of its ministers—sanctified and rejoiced in the conquests of the flag, and encouraged, if it did not formulate, the belief that conquest, with the resulting relative well-being of the

Western populations, was proof of the favor of God. God had come a long way from the desert—but then so had Allah, though in a very different direction. God, going north, and rising on the wings of power, had become white, and Allah, out of power, and on the dark side of Heaven, had become—for all practical purposes, anyway—black. Thus, in the realm of morals the role of Christianity has been, at best, ambivalent. Even leaving out of account the remarkable arrogance that assumed that the ways and morals of others were inferior to those of Christians, and that they therefore had every right, and could use any means, to change them, the collision between cultures—and the schizophrenia in the mind of Christendom—had rendered the domain of morals as chartless as the sea once was, and as treacherous as the sea still is. It is not too much to say that whoever wishes to become a truly moral human being (and let us not ask whether or not this is possible; I think we must *believe* that it is possible) must first divorce himself from all the prohibitions, crimes, and hypocrisies of the Christian church. If the concept of God has any validity or any use, it can only be to make us larger, freer, and more loving. If God cannot do this, then it is time we got rid of Him.

This superb instance of Baldwin's stance and style as a moral essayist depends for its rhetorical power upon a judicious blend of excess and restraint. Its crucial sentence achieves prophetic authority:

It is not too much to say that whoever wishes to become a truly moral human being (and let us not ask whether or not this is possible; I think we must *believe* that it is possible) must first divorce himself from all the prohibitions, crimes, and hypocrisies of the Christian church.

The parenthesis, nobly skeptical, is the trope of a master rhetorician, and placing "believe" in italics nicely puts into question the problematics of faith. "Divorce," denounced by St. Paul as having been introduced because of our hardness of hearts, acquires the antithetical aura of the Church itself, while Christian prohibitions are assimilated (rather wickedly) to Christian crimes and hypocrisies. This is, rhetorically considered, good, unclean fun, but the burden is savage, and steeped in moral high seriousness. The strength of *The Fire Next Time* comes to rest in its final paragraph, with the interplay between two italicized rhetorical questions, an interplay kindled when *"then"* is added to the second question:

> When I was very young, and was dealing with my buddies in those wine- and urine-stained hallways, something in me wondered, *What will happen to all that beauty?* For black people, though I am aware that some of us, black and white, do not know it yet, are very beautiful. And when I sat at Elijah's table and watched the baby, the women, and the men, and we talked about God's—or Allah's—vengeance, I wondered, when that vengeance was achieved, *What will happen to all that beauty then?* I could also see that the intransigence and ignorance of the white world might make that vengeance inevitable—a vengeance that does not really depend on, and cannot really be executed by, any person or organization, and that cannot be prevented by any police force or army: historical vengeance, a cosmic vengeance, based on the law that we recognize when we say, "Whatever goes up must come down." And here we are, at the center of the arc, trapped in the gaudiest, most valuable, and most improbable water wheel the world has ever seen. Everything now, we must assume, is in our hands; we have no right to assume otherwise. If we—and now I mean the relatively conscious whites and the relatively conscious blacks, who must, like lovers, insist on, or create, the consciousness of the others—do not falter in our duty now, we may be able, handful that we are, to end the racial nightmare, and achieve our country, and change the history of the world. If we do not now dare everything, the fulfillment of that prophecy, recreated from the Bible in song by a slave, is upon us: "God gave Noah the rainbow sign, No more water, the fire next time!"

The shrewd rhetorical movement here is from the waterwheel to the ambivalent divine promise of no second flood, the promise of covenant with its dialectical countersong of the conflagration ensuing from our violation of covenant. That vision of impending fire re-illuminates the poignant question: *"What will happen to all that beauty then?"* All that beauty that is in jeopardy transcends even the beauty of black people, and extends to everything human, and to bird, beast, and flower.

No Name in the Street takes its fierce title from Job 18:16–19, where it is spoken to Job by Bildad the Shuhite, concerning the fate of the wicked:

> His roots shall be dried up beneath, and above shall his branch be cut off.
>
> His remembrance shall perish from the earth, and he shall have no name in the street.
>
> He shall be driven from light into darkness, and chased out of the world.
>
> He shall neither have son nor nephew among his people, nor any remaining in his dwellings.
>
> They that come after him shall be astonished at his day, as they that went before were affrighted.

I have to admit, having just read (and re-read) my way through the 690 pages of *The Price of the Ticket*, that frequently I am tempted to reply to Baldwin with Job's response to Bildad:

> How long will ye vex my soul, and break me in pieces with words?
>
> These ten times have ye reproached me: ye are not ashamed that ye make yourselves strange to me. And be it indeed that I have erred, mine error remaineth with myself.
>
> If indeed ye will magnify yourselves against me, and plead against me my reproach.

Baldwin's rhetorical authority as prophet would be seriously impaired if he were merely Job's comforter, Bildad rather than Jeremiah. *No Name in the Street* cunningly evades the risk that Baldwin will magnify himself against the reader, partly by the book's adroitness at stationing the author himself in the vulnerable contexts of his own existence, both in New York and in Paris. By not allowing himself (or his readers) to forget how perpetually a black homosexual aesthete and moralist, writer and preacher, must fight for his life, Baldwin earns the pathos of the prophetic predicament:

> I made such motions as I could to understand what was happening, and to keep myself afloat. But I had been away too long. It was not only that I could not readjust myself to life in New York—it was also that I would not: I was never going to be anybody's nigger again. But I was now to discover that the world has more than one way of keeping you a nigger, has evolved more than one way of skinning the cat; if the hand slips here, it tightens there, and now I was offered, gracefully indeed: membership in the club. I had lunch at some elegant bistros, dinner at some exclusive clubs. I tried to be understanding about my countrymen's concern for difficult me, and unruly mine—and I really was trying to be understanding, though not without some bewilderment, and, eventually, some malice. I began to be profoundly uncomfortable. It was a strange kind of discomfort, a terrified apprehension that I had lost my bearings. I did not altogether understand what I was hearing. I did not trust what I heard myself saying. In very little that I heard did I hear anything that reflected anything which I knew, or had endured, of life. My mother and my father, my brothers and my sisters were not present at the tables at which I sat down, and no one in the company had ever heard of them. My own beginnings, or instincts, began to shift as nervously as the cigarette smoke that wavered around my head. I was not trying to hold on to my wretchedness. On the contrary, if my poverty was coming, at last, to an end, so much the better, and it wasn't happening a moment too soon—and yet, I felt an increasing chill, as though the rest of my life would have to be lived in silence.

The discomfort of having lost bearings is itself a prophetic trope, and comes to its fruition in the book's searing final paragraph:

> To be an Afro-American, or an American black, is to be in the situation, intolerably exaggerated, of all those who have ever found themselves part of a civilization which they could in no

way honorably defend—which they were compelled, indeed, endlessly to attack and condemn—and who yet spoke out of the most passionate love, hoping to make the kingdom new, to make it honorable and worthy of life. Whoever is part of whatever civilization helplessly loves some aspects of it, and some of the people in it. A person does not lightly elect to oppose his society. One would much rather be at home among one's compatriots than be mocked and detested by them. And there is a level on which the mockery of the people, even their hatred, is moving because it is so blind: it is terrible to watch people cling to their captivity and insist on their own destruction. I think black people have always felt this about America, and Americans, and have always seen, spinning above the thoughtless American head, the shape of the wrath to come.

Not to be at home among one's compatriots is to avoid the catastrophe of being at ease in the new Zion that is America. A reader, however moved by Baldwin's rhetorical authority, can be disturbed here by the implication that all blacks are prophets, at least in our society. Would to God indeed that all the Lord's people were prophets, but they are not, and cannot be.

III

Like every true prophet, Baldwin passionately would prefer the fate of Jonah to that of Jeremiah, but I do not doubt that his authentic descent from Jeremiah will continue to be valid until well after the end of his life (and mine). The final utterance in *The Price of the Ticket* seems to me Baldwin's most poignant, ever:

Freaks are called freaks and are treated as they are treated— in the main, abominably—because they are human beings who cause to echo, deep within us, our most profound terrors and desires.

Most of us, however, do not appear to be freaks—though we are rarely what we appear to be. We are, for the most part, visibly male or female, our social roles defined by our sexual equipment.

But we are all androgynous, not only because we are all
born of a woman impregnated by the seed of a man but
because each of us, helplessly and forever, contains the
other—male in female, female in male, white in black and
black in white. We are a part of each other. Many of my
countrymen appear to find this fact exceedingly inconvenient
and even unfair, and so, very often, do I. But none of us can
do anything about it.

Baldwin is most prophetic, and most persuasive, when his voice is
as subdued as it is here. What gives the rhetorical effect of self-subdual
is the precise use of plural pronouns throughout. Moving from his own
predicament to the universal, the prophet achieves an effect directly
counter to Jeremiah's pervasive trope of individualizing the prophetic
alternative. The ultimate tribute that Baldwin has earned is his authentic
share in Jeremiah's most terrible utterance:

O Lord, thou has deceived me, and I was deceived: thou art
stronger than I, and hast prevailed: I am in derision daily,
every one mocketh me.
    For since I spake, I cried out, I cried violence and spoil;
because the word of the Lord was made a reproach unto me,
and a derision, daily.
    Then I said, I will not make mention of him, nor speak
any more in his name. But his word was in mine heart as a
burning fire shut up in my bones, and I was weary with
forbearing, and I could not stay.

AMY SICKELS

Biography of James Baldwin

THE WEIGHT OF WHITE PEOPLE

When he was nineteen years old, James Baldwin entered a restaurant in New Jersey with a white friend, and a counterman stopped him from ordering: "We don't serve Negroes here." Baldwin had heard this line before, but this time, something in him snapped. He stormed out of the restaurant and began wandering the streets of New Jersey, his rage growing.

> The streets were very crowded and I was facing north. People were moving in every direction but it seemed to me, in that instant, that all of the people I could see, and many more than that, were moving toward me, against me, and that everyone was white. I remember how their faces gleamed. And I felt, like a physical sensation, a *click* at the nape of my neck as though some interior string connecting my head to my body had been cut.... I wanted to do something to crush these white faces, which were crushing me. (*Notes of a Native Son* 96)

Feeling worked up, Baldwin went into an expensive restaurant where he knew he would not be served. He sat down at an empty table, and after a few minutes, a young waitress came over and recited the same refrain, with a note of apology in her voice.

"I hated her for her white face, and for her great, astounded, frightened eyes," admitted Baldwin. "I felt that if she found a black man so frightening I would make her fright worth-while" (*Notes of a Native Son* 96). In that instant, Baldwin hurled a glass of water at the young woman. She ducked, and the glass smashed against the mirror behind the bar. Suddenly, Baldwin realized what he'd done. A man grabbed him, but he kicked loose and heard his friend yelling for him to "Run!"

Baldwin escaped, but he never forgot the intense feelings of fear and hatred: "I could not get over two facts, both equally difficult for the imagination to grasp, and one was that I could have been murdered. But the other was that I had been ready to commit murder. I saw nothing very clearly but I did see this: that my life, my *real* life, was in danger and not from anything other people might do but from the hatred I carried in my own heart" (*Notes of a Native Son* 98).

This dramatic event served as a turning point in Baldwin's life, in which he challenged himself "to keep my own heart free of hatred and despair," despite the crushing prevalence and power of racism in America (*Notes of a Native Son* 114). He had grown up witnessing his father's hatred toward the white world, and Baldwin knew that in order to survive, he must rise above this feeling of hopelessness. He realized that in order to not be defeated, he needed to examine both himself and the country that produced such terror and violence. This experience signaled a profound revelation for Baldwin, which was to serve as a foundation for his personal, political, and artistic philosophy for the next forty years. Although he did not yet realize it, he had discovered his true writing subject: himself and America.

The struggle to keep his heart free of hatred was not an easy task. As a gay, black man, James Baldwin faced many prejudices throughout his life, and he lived during one of the most politically explosive times in modern American history—in which the Civil Rights Movement rose up against the segregation, violence, and racism that dominated the American South. In order to realize his own complicated relationship to America, Baldwin discovered he needed to leave—and he spent all of his adult life moving back and forth between Paris and New York.

In the 1950s and 60s, Baldwin became more active in the growing Civil Rights Movement, and with eloquent essays such as "Down at the Cross," he quickly captured the attention of the American public. Although Baldwin claimed he did not want to be a spokesman, he did not shirk from the spotlight when America turned to him for guidance and for a better understanding of the relationship between whites and blacks. Baldwin gave many lectures and interviews, and he was a fiery, moving speaker—but it was his writing that truly depicted his unstoppable fire. Baldwin left behind a rich collection of fiction and nonfiction that captured the danger of a divided America, writing that challenged both whites and blacks to reach out to each other. Works such as *Notes of a Native Son*, *Go Tell It On The Mountain*, *Giovanni's Room*, *Another Country*, and *The Fire Next Time*—all which helped to establish Baldwin's esteemed literary reputation—penetrated the walls of myth to reach the truth and complexity of human experiences and relationships.

Baldwin believed that a writer must write out of his experience and act as a ruthlessly perceptive witness to the world around him—to depict the world with honesty and complexity. He explained that he became a subject for his work because "I was the only witness I had" (*Conversations* 276). Baldwin's personal experience of the world included growing up in Harlem, learning what it meant to be an artist in Greenwich Village, and discovering his American identity in Paris. Although he was split between all of these places, in his writing he managed to connect them—as he did the many other splintered aspects of his identity.

In both his personal life and his writing, Baldwin defied neat categories and labels. His work conveyed the perspective of gay, straight, black, and white people—and yet all of these views were born from one man's vision of the world. Americans needed to examine themselves deeply, he insisted, "to trust your experience" and "know whence you came," in order for the country to survive (*The Fire Next Time* 8).

In his own life, he managed to overcome the hatred, despite the difficult experience of feeling "the weight of white people in the world" (*Notes of a Native Son* 88). Even after the Civil Rights Movement ended and his political views grew more radical, Baldwin's overall message of love never disappeared—love, regardless of gender, was what could save America. Baldwin never claimed that his hope for the world was easy to attain—he realized the difficulty, the struggle. Yet through all of the pain and despair, he did not turn his back on his true subject: he experienced the world fully, and wrote everything down: "All art is a kind of confession, more or less oblique," he once wrote. "All artists, if they are to survive, are forced, at last, to tell the whole story; to vomit the anguish up."

DISCOVERIES OF CHILDHOOD

James Arthur Baldwin was born on August 2, 1924, to Emma Berdis Jones and an unknown father in the Harlem Hospital, at 135 Street and Lenox Avenue, in New York City.

Emma Berdis Jones, who was nineteen when she gave birth to Baldwin, arrived in New York from Deals Island, Maryland, after World War I, when waves of African-Americans were fleeing the southern states for the promise of the North. Her mother died when Berdis was a young girl, and she lived with her father, a fisherman. Like many African-Americans during the time, Berdis went North in hopes of finding a better life.

Berdis never revealed the identity of Baldwin's biological father to him, and she refused to answer his questions about how difficult it must have been for her—to be living alone in Harlem, as a single mother, during the 1920s. When he was a teenager, Baldwin found out that he had been born illegitimate, which haunted him for much of his life.

When Baldwin was three years old, Berdis married David Baldwin, the only father Baldwin ever knew and one of the most significant influences on his life. A Baptist minister and laborer, David Baldwin arrived to the North from New Orleans in 1919. Baldwin never knew the exact age of his step-father, except that he was much older than his mother. David had born near the end of the Civil War and was the son of a slave, Barbara, who had given birth to fourteen children, some of whom were "black" and some "white." Barbara Baldwin lived with her son's family in Harlem until her death in 1930, when James Baldwin was seven years old. It was from his grandmother that he first heard stories of slavery and the South.

Both of Baldwin's parents had experienced difficult lives, but they endured these struggles differently—his mother with a quiet strength, his father with an angry bitterness. Berdis strove to instill the power of love and family in her children, urging them, as brothers and sisters, to always take care of one another. She provided her children with love in rough, uncertain times: "I think she saved us all," Baldwin once said. "She was the only person in the world we could turn to, yet she couldn't protect us" (*Conversations* 77). David Baldwin, on the other hand, showed his wife and children little affection. Although he occasionally tried to connect with his children, as Baldwin recalled in "Notes of a Native Son," it was rarely with any success: "When he took one of his children on his knee to play, the child always became fretful and began to cry; when he tried to help one of us with our homework the absolutely unabating tension which emanated from him caused our minds and our tongues to become paralyzed, so that he, scarcely knowing why, flew into a rage and the child, not knowing why, was punished" (*Conversations* 88).

The Baldwin household often erupted with beatings and furious arguments, an atmosphere that resulted from David's terrible temper colliding with the impoverished living conditions. The many apartments the Baldwins lived in were essentially the same: dilapidated and overcrowded. The lack of food, hot water, and heat contributed to the chaotic atmosphere. The Great Depression, beginning in 1929, and the frequent job lay-offs, made it more difficult for David to provide for his family. Furthermore, racism dominated the American workforce, and very few employment opportunities existed for blacks. For years David took a train every day from Harlem to Long Island to work at a soft drink bottling factory, while Berdis cleaned houses and took in laundry for whites. Although David and Berdis worked constantly, it was difficult to earn enough to make ends meet, especially as their family continued to expand. Together, David and Berdis would have eight children—three boys and five girls. In addition, one of David's sons from a previous marriage lived with the family until his father's anger finally drove him away. Later, Baldwin recalled often feeling hungry as a child. Sometimes the family subsisted on nothing but cans of corned beef and stewed prunes donated from home-relief workers. When he was older, Baldwin realized much of his father's anger must have stemmed from this: "I began to wonder what it could have felt like for such a man to have had nine children whom he could barely feed" (*Notes of a Native Son* 90).

In an effort to find cheaper living, the Baldwin family was forced to move frequently to different apartments, but they always lived in Harlem, between Lenox Avenue on the west and the Harlem River on the east, and between 130th and 135th Streets. During this time, Harlem was not overwhelmed by the projects and slums that threatened to destroy the neighborhood in later years; however, the early signs of dilapidation were already present in the crumbling buildings and dirty streets. In the area where the Baldwin family lived, poverty set them apart from the wealthier Harlem blocks. "You see, there were two Harlems where we lived. There was a great divide between the black people on the Hill and us. I was just a ragged, funky black shoeshine boy and was afraid of the people on the Hill, who, for their part, didn't want to have anything to do with me" (*Conversations* 223). In his essay "The Harlem Ghetto" Baldwin observes that all over Harlem "there is felt the same bitter expectancy with which, in my childhood, we awaited winter: it is coming and it will be hard; there is nothing anyone can do about it" (57). Baldwin's description of the "sense of congestion, rather like the insistent, maddening, claustrophobic pounding in the skull that comes from trying to breath in a very small room with all the windows shut" also characterizes the cramped Baldwin household (57).

With such a large family and tight quarters, it was often difficult to find privacy. Perhaps this intimate atmosphere, established so early in his life, contributed to Baldwin's need to be surrounded by others—he always had brothers, sisters, and his father's mother, Barbara, around. Bed-ridden and feeble, Barbara helped protect Baldwin—scolding her son when he treated Baldwin badly. But this lack of privacy could also be stifling—especially with the overbearing presence of his father. David Baldwin was not gentle with any of his children, but he was especially cruel toward his step-son, calling him ugly and "frog eyes." He made Baldwin self-conscious about his looks, and throughout his adult life, Baldwin's dark skin, large eyes, and slight build would be a source of insecurity. Once, when he was a boy, Baldwin looked out the window and saw a women with thick lips and big eyes, similar to his own, and he called to his mother, "Look, there someone who's uglier than you and me" (Campbell 7). As a child, Baldwin was timid and shy, and fearful of his father. Beatings and threats were common. Once, during an extremely cold winter, David gave Baldwin his last dime to go to the store for kerosene for the stove, but Baldwin slipped on the icy street and lost the dime. According to his biographer W.J. Weatherby, David punished Baldwin by beating him with an iron cord until he was half-conscious.

A small, somewhat effeminate, and frail child, Baldwin learned early on that it was his mind that would help him survive—words, not muscles, would be his strength. He was highly intelligent and imaginative, and when he started school at P.S. 249, in 1929, the year of the Great Crash, he found the outlet he needed—a temporary relief from home, and an introduction into a world beyond Harlem. He was often mocked by the other school children for his small size and ragged clothes, but books became Baldwin's solace, his escape from insults and the demands of his father. A precocious and curious child, he always had a book in hand, and as he grew older and helped his mother take care of the younger children, he continued to make time for reading: "As they were born, I took them over with one hand and held a book with the other" (*Notes of a Native Son* 3). Baldwin already knew the Bible well— from the readings that had been proscribed by his father and would later influence his writing style—and before he was in high school, he had read Dickens and Dostoevsky. He read the abolitionist Harriet Beecher Stowe's *Uncle Tom's Cabin*, one of his favorite books, when he was around seven or eight years old, and he also started writing songs, stories, and plays at an early age, and "began plotting novels at about the time I learned to read" (3).

Over the course of his childhood, Baldwin encountered several mentors, but two of his earliest influences were the principal of P.S. 24, Mrs. Gertrude Ayer, the first black principal in New York City, and his sixth grade teacher, Orilla "Bill" Miller, a young white woman who encouraged his creative talents and introduced him to the world of theater. In the Baldwin household, theater, movies, and non-religious music were forbidden, but Miller, possibly because she was white, was able to overcome David Baldwin's objections. One of the most memorable outings Miller took Baldwin on was to see the Orson Welles' production of *Macbeth*, set in Haiti and with an all black cast, at the Lafayette Theater on 132nd Street. Miller and Baldwin remained close for a few years after he left her class, and, during a particularly rough winter, she helped out his family with donations of food and supplies.

In 1936, Baldwin continued his literary endeavors when he enrolled in Frederick Douglass Junior High, where the renown Harlem Renaissance poet Countee Cullen taught French, and another influential teacher, Herman Porter, introduced Baldwin to the New York public library on 42nd Street, where Baldwin researched a paper he was writing on Harlem. Once, when Porter arrived at the Baldwins' to pick up his student, he was, like Baldwin's school teacher Orilla Miller, appalled by the extent of the family's poverty. David Baldwin accused Porter of trying to corrupt his son with books by "white devils," but begrudgingly gave his consent for the field trip. While books provided Baldwin with a feeling of freedom, his father often flared up at the sight of them, and viewed all books, except the Bible, with deep suspicion.

While novels and stories helped Baldwin to temporarily retreat from the domineering presence of his father, they could not help him escape the cruelty of racism: "[T]he most difficult (and most rewarding) thing in my life has been the fact that I was born a Negro and was forced, therefore, to effect some kind of truce with this reality" (*Notes of a Native Son* 5). In the vicinity of Harlem where he lived, the population was made up of predominately African-Americans, except for the Jewish store owners, who Baldwin later defended: "But just as a society must have a scapegoat, so hatred must have a symbol. Georgia has the Negro and Harlem has the Jew" (*Notes of a Native Son* 72). The only other white people he encountered were welfare workers, bill collectors, and the police—with whom he had two encounters when he was young. Once, when he was ten years old, two white policemen intimidated and frisked him, and then left him, terrified, flat on his back in an empty lot. Another time, when he went alone to the 42nd street library because he'd already read everything in the Harlem branch, a policeman stopped him: "Why don't you niggers stay uptown where you belong?" (*The Fire Next Time* 19).

These incidents left deep impressions on Baldwin, and he could conceive of "no Negro native to this country who has not, by the age of puberty, been irreparably scarred by the conditions of his life" (*Notes of a Native Son* 71). Early on, Baldwin understood that his world in Harlem was much different, and separate, from the places where whites lived. But there was one spot where Baldwin could see both worlds. He had a favorite hill in Central Park, where he could look one way to see Harlem, and look the other way to see downtown, the two worlds of black and white, both of which would become inseparable from his life.

BORN AGAIN

In facing this perpetual struggle against poverty and racism, many Harlem residents found solace and hope in the church. Harlem was filled with Baptist and Pentecostal churches, many of which were created when the first wave of black immigrants arrived from the South after the First World War, bringing with them their strong community values and religious beliefs. "I was born into a Southern community displaced into the streets of New York," Baldwin once said. "And what did we bring with us? What did my father bring with him? He brought with him his

Bible" (Campbell 9). Many congregations did not meet in traditional churches, which would have been too expensive, but congregated wherever they could find a place—in basements, apartments, or storefronts.

Baldwin's mother was a devout Christian, and whenever his father was not working at the bottle factory, he preached fiery sermons in Pentecostal storefront churches, which Baldwin evocatively depicts in his first novel *Go Tell It On The Mountain*. Proudly dressed in a three piece suit, with cufflinks and spats, David Baldwin embraced religion with fervor, as it gave him a voice to rise above the overwhelming obstacles he and other African-Americans faced. As Baldwin pointed out, his father "had already suffered many kinds of ruin; in his outrageously demanding and protective way he loved his children who were black and menaced like him" (*Notes of a Native Son* 87). David's devotion to God was united with the hope that God would take revenge on white "devils." Although at the time Baldwin found his father only to be cruel and bitter, when he was older, he explored the complexity of his father's strict religious beliefs, how David's fear and dislike of whites rose from the way he had been treated like a second-class citizen all of his life:

> He could be chilling in the pulpit and indescribably cruel in his personal life and he was certainly the most bitter man I have ever met; yet it must be said that there was something else in him, buried in him, which lent him his tremendous power and, even, a rather crushing charm. It had something to do with his blackness, I think—he was very black—with his blackness and his beauty, and with the fact that he knew that he was black but did not know that he was beautiful. (87)

Struggling to provide for his family against a crushing wave of racism, David Baldwin had little self-confidence, but in the pulpit, "like a prophet," he turned his despair into anger and fiery sermons (89). David railed against whites in his sermons, but his stepson noticed whenever his father encountered them in real life—landlords and bill collectors— he was bitterly subordinate. This familiar scene—his father's bitter subservience—incited Baldwin as a young teen to feel disrespect and contempt toward him. Later, in his essay "My Dungeon Shook" he wrote that his father "had a terrible life; he was defeated long before he died because, at the bottom of his heart, he really believed what white people said about him. This is one of the reasons that he became so holy" (4).

Although his father's influence over his family was powerful, Baldwin never fully accepted his father's extreme views. But, like his father, Baldwin did enthusiastically embrace the church—just not his father's. At fourteen, Baldwin, in the midst of the rising confusion of puberty, the ongoing conflicts with his father, and the struggle of trying to find a place to fit in, turned to God: "I underwent, during the summer that I became fourteen, a prolonged religious crisis" (*The Fire Next Time* 15).

By the time he was a teenager, Harlem was sliding more quickly into despair. Baldwin witnessed friends and neighbors turn to drugs and alcohol, and inevitably give up on life. All around him he saw drug addicts, pimps, and prostitutes, as people in the neighborhood searched for an escape from the endless oppression:

> Just before and then during the Second World War, many of my friends fled into the service, all to be changed there, and rarely for the better, many to be ruined, and many to die. Others fled to other states and cities—that is, to other ghettos. Some went on wine or whiskey or the needle, and are still on it. And others, like me, fled into the church. (*The Fire Next Time* 20)

Baldwin's fears and insecurities "rose up like a wall between the world and me, and drove me into the church" (27).

That summer, Baldwin went with a friend to Mount Calvary, a Pentecostal church, also known as "Mother Horn's church." When Baldwin met the pastor, Mother Horn, he immediately felt a sense of belonging: "It was my good luck—perhaps—that I found myself in the church racket instead of some other, and surrendered to a spiritual seduction long before I came to any carnal knowledge. For when the pastor asked me, with that marvelous smile, "Whose little boy are you?" my heart replied at once, "Why, yours" (*The Fire Next Time* 29).

The church gave Baldwin a sense of identity and of belonging— something every teenager struggles to find. As a young man approaching puberty, he felt overwhelmed by his feelings of desire and sexuality, which he believed were sinful, and he also feared that he was attracted to boys as well as girls. In this guilt-ridden state, he underwent the radical experience of being "born again:"

> The summer wore on, and things got worse. I became more guilty and more frightened, and kept all this bottled up inside me, and naturally, inescapably, one night, when this woman had finished preaching, everything came roaring, screaming, crying out, and I fell to the ground before the alter. It was the strangest sensation I have ever had in my life—up to that time, or since. (*The Fire Next Time* 29)

Shortly after this, Baldwin went to a smaller church, the Fireside Pentecostal Assembly, where he started preaching at age fourteen. Many years later, Baldwin would move audiences with his passionate speeches on Civil Rights, race relations, and American identity, but it was in church that he first learned how to use rhetoric effectively. Through his sermons, he lost his shyness and became a performer, learning about cadence, measured speech, and the power a public speaker could wield over a crowd. Because of his young age and exuberance, Baldwin's sermons drew bigger crowds than his father's, which delighted him.

As Baldwin became more involved with the church, his relationship with his father changed, but instead of religion bringing them closer, the distance between them grew. Once Baldwin had cowered in fear, but his role as a Young Minster inspired him to be bolder. He now had something that his father could not take away from him, and his devotion to the church allowed him to have more time to himself. He preached at least one sermon per week, which meant "that there were hours and even whole days when I could not be interrupted—not even by my father. I had immobilized him." Many years later he realized, "I had also immobilized myself, and had escaped from nothing whatever" (*The Fire Next Time* 33).

Baldwin stayed in the pulpit for more than three years. Although he invested most of time and energy in the church, he did not drop out of school, as his father advised him to do. In 1938, Baldwin was accepted to the prestigious De Witt Clinton High School in the Bronx, situated on a long, tree-lined avenue. The neighborhood was populated by immigrants, most of them Jewish and nearly everyone white. This crucial experience set in place a division, a push and pull that Baldwin would struggle with throughout his life. In this case, he felt torn between religion and art. When he was at home, Baldwin devoted his time to the church, but at De Witt, he was friends with artists and writers, including Richard Avedon, who later became an internationally famous photographer, and Emile Capouya and Sol Stein, who both became well-known literary editors.

In both the pulpit and at school, Baldwin was popular, winning people over with his charm and persuasiveness. He was wiry, witty, argumentative, and ambitious. Although the majority of the students at De Witt were white, and none were as poor as Baldwin, he had many friends and he was generally well-liked. Baldwin worked on the school magazine, *The Magpie*, to which he regularly contributed plays, poems, stories, and he was known by his teachers and peers to be one of the brighter students.

Eventually, Baldwin felt pushed to make a decision between the two contradicting parts of his life—between art and religion, his sexuality and the church. However, it was not easy to leave the church, which had provided Baldwin with a startling feeling of invigoration and exhilaration. "The church was very exciting. It took a long time for me to disengage myself from this excitement, and on the blindest, most visceral level, I never really have, and never will," he wrote in "Down at the Cross." "There is no music like that music, no drama like the drama of the saints rejoicing, the sinners moaning, the tambourines racing, and all those voices coming together and crying holy unto the Lord" (33).

However, in the end, books, films, and theater appealed to him more than sermons. According to Baldwin, he began to lose his faith in religion "when I began to read again" (*The Fire Next Time* 34). In addition to his love for literature, theater, and films, the new friendships he had formed also played a part in his decision to leave the church. Most of his new friends were Jewish, and he felt conflicted by what he began to see as the church's hypocrisy. Baldwin recalled that when he told his father that his best friend was Jewish, his father slapped him "all the hatred and all the fear, and the depth of a merciless resolve to kill me—and I knew that all of those sermons and tears and all that repentance and rejoicing had changed nothing" (37). For all of Baldwin's childhood, his father had pointed out to him that as a black boy, he would find nothing but misery and hardship in the world. He warned him that his "white friends in high school were not really my friends and that I would see, when I was older, how white people would do anything to keep a Negro down" (*Notes of a Native Son* 92). At the time, Baldwin dismissed him, but a few years later, he would reconsider his father's beliefs and wonder how he could stop himself from being eaten up by the same anger and bitterness.

Other significant events that occurred during this time also contributed to Baldwin leaving the church, one of which was the major discovery that he was not the biological son of David Baldwin. One day, around the age of sixteen, Baldwin was sitting on a park bench with his friend Emile Capouya, when he burst into tears and revealed he had just overheard a conversation and learned that he was illegitimate. Although Baldwin may have suspected this for some time, hearing the truth had shattered him. "He was very emotional, very tearful," Capouya told Weatherby (Weatherby 6). This momentous discovery furthered complicated Baldwin's tumultuous relationship with his father, and caused him more anxiety about his identity. In addition to this revelation, Baldwin was also struggling with his sexuality, and his yearning to live the life of an artist. At the age of sixteen, Baldwin made a life-changing decision. His final sermon was "Set thy house in order," his father's favorite verse. Immediately afterwards, Baldwin went with Capouya to a matinee at 42nd Street. The choice had been made: art over religion.

LEARNING TO SEE

Another major influence in Baldwin's decision to forgo religion for the life of the artist was meeting the painter Beauford Delaney, who would later win considerable prestige for his portraits of African-Americans, including Ella Fitzgerald, Duke Ellington, W.E.B. Du Bois, and W.C. Handy. A year before Baldwin left the church, Capouya introduced him to Delaney, who lived in Greenwich Village. With the exception of Baldwin's brief encounter with Countee Cullen in junior high, Beauford Delaney was the first successful, self-supporting black artist Baldwin had ever met, proof to Baldwin that he could live this unconventional kind of life. The thirty-nine year old Delaney took fifteen-year-old Baldwin under his wing and was one of the most important influences in his life. Delaney became a father-figure for

Baldwin, and Baldwin remained his devoted "son"—many years later, when Delaney was ill, Baldwin helped him find the care he needed. Their close friendship lasted forty years, until Delaney's death in 1979.

At his studio at 181 Greene Street, Delaney introduced Baldwin to blues and jazz, music that was forbidden in the Baldwin household. They listened to recordings of Ella Fitzgerald, Fats Waller, and Bessie Smith. Delaney exposed Baldwin to art galleries and concerts, introduced him to his wide circle of artistic friends, and most importantly, convinced Baldwin to trust his artistic consciousness. Although at the time Baldwin was still unsure of his sexuality, it was also important for him to have Delaney—a successful gay, black artist—as a role model. In *Talking at the Gates*, Baldwin's biographer James Campbell stresses the importance of Delaney's influence on Baldwin: "Delaney was important not only for his aesthetic teaching, but for the precedent Baldwin found in his way of living. Delaney was neither famous nor rich; yet he was incontrovertibly an artist. And although he was a black artist, his work was not complicated—or simplified—by matters of protest. He tried above all to do his duty as a painter: to see clearly and to put down what he saw, to bear witness" (Campbell 21).

Baldwin credited Delaney for one of his most important lessons in becoming a writer—learning to see. He remembered standing on a street corner with Delaney, waiting for the light to change, and Delaney pointed and said, "Look." Baldwin saw a puddle of water. "Look again," Delaney told him. This time, Baldwin saw oil on the water and the city reflected in the puddle. "It was a great revelation to me. I can't explain it. He taught me how to see, and how to trust what I saw. Painters have often taught writers how to see. And once you've had that experience, you can see differently," he said in an interview with the *Paris Review* (*Conversations* 235).

Despite all of his confusion about religion, race, and his relationship with his father, one certainty that became more clear and definite to Baldwin was that he wanted to become a writer. In his high school yearbook, next to his picture, Baldwin stated his goal was to become "a novelist/playwright: Fame is the spur and—ouch!" (Campbell 23). In one of the few "real" conversations Baldwin recalled having with his father, "the one time in all our life together when we had really spoken to each other" his father asked if it was true he would rather write than preach. "I was astonished at his question—because it was a real question," Baldwin later admitted. "I answered, "Yes." That was all we said. It was awful to remember that was all we had *ever* said" (*Notes of a Native Son* 108).

To find success as a writer, Baldwin believed he needed to leave Harlem. Although Harlem had thrived with arts during the Harlem Renaissance, this period had peaked during Baldwin's childhood and had never been a part of Baldwin's life as a writer. Downtown Greenwich Village beckoned him, as it did many young artists, writers, and bohemians. Although Baldwin already spent most of his free time there, he could not yet make the move permanent—as the eldest child in the family, he needed to earn a living and help his parents feed his siblings.

Although Baldwin was extremely bright, his grades were never high and college did not interest him. At the end of his high school graduation in 1941, which coincided roughly with the entry of United States into WWII, Capouya helped Baldwin get a job at a defense plant in Belle Mead, New Jersey. The wages were good, $80 per week, but the work was physically exhausting, especially for a man of Baldwin's size—as an adult, he was slight, and stood 5'6". He was not a devoted employee, and was fired and rehired a few times.

It was not only the job he disliked—it was also the place. Although he was no stranger to racism, Baldwin felt shocked by the level of hostility in New Jersey, where racism and segregation were far more blatant than in New York City: "I learned in New Jersey that to be a Negro meant, precisely, that one was never looked at but was simply at the mercy of the reflexes of one's skin caused in other people" (*Notes of a Native Son* 93). Whenever he went out to eat with his co-workers, he was told he had to leave because of the color of his skin. His anger and disgust slowly built up, until one night, after quitting his job, he reached the breaking point that significantly affected his views on race and identity—in which the familiar line, "We don't serve Negroes here" set him off in a fury that frightened him.

After that night of throwing the glass at the white waitress, Baldwin took a long, hard look at his emotions. The anger and hatred that filled Baldwin frightened him, and he inevitably compared himself to his father. Baldwin had been away from home for a year, and in that year, "I had time to become aware of the meaning of all my father's bitter warnings, had discovered the secret of his proudly pursed lips and rigid carriage: I had discovered the weight of white people in the world" (*Notes of a Native Son* 88).

Baldwin believed that it was his father's bitterness and anger that contributed to the rapid deterioration of his health. Bitter, defeated, and ill with tuberculosis, David eventually lost his mind. "We had not known that he was being eaten up by paranoia, and the discovery that his cruelty, to our bodies and our minds, had been one of the symptoms of his illness was not, then, enough to enable us to forgive him," explained Baldwin (*Notes of a Native Son* 89). His father became less aware of the world around him and declined into dementia. One night he left the house and wandered the streets, until Baldwin found him on a park bench, staring at nothing. Blinded by paranoia, David refused to eat because he thought his family was trying to poison him. Finally, he was committed to an institution on Long Island, where he was fed intravenously.

Baldwin was too upset at seeing his father in this helpless condition. He only visited David once in the hospital, which happened to be for "the first time during his illness and for the last time in his life" (*Notes of a Native Son* 101). In his famous essay "Notes to a Native Son," Baldwin described the anger, grief, and guilt that he felt:

> I had told my mother that I did not want to see him because I hated him. But this was not true. It was only that I had hated him and I wanted to hold onto this hatred. I did not want to look on him as a ruin: it was not a ruin that I had hated. I imagine that one of the reasons people cling to their hates so stubbornly is because they sense, once hate is gone, that they will be forced to deal with pain. (101)

When he saw his father in the hospital, Baldwin was shocked by how small and harmless he looked, and he was overwhelmed with feelings of compassion: "I wanted to take his hand, to say something" (103). But instead, he left without touching his father.

The day after the visit, on July 29, 1943, David Baldwin died, and that same day, Berdis gave birth to their last child, Paula. The day of David's funeral fell on Baldwin's nineteenth birthday, and caused him profound grief and sadness. He returned to Harlem for the funeral, and was upset by the changes he saw in the neighborhood—the slums, the oppressive police presence. On the afternoon of the funeral, a major riot broke out in Harlem, after a rumor started (which was not correct in its details) that a white policeman had shot a black soldier at the Hotel Braddock on 125th Street. Angry mobs attacked and looted white-owned businesses, and for Baldwin, the chaotic setting only reinforced his own jumbled emotions: "As we drove him to the graveyard, the spoils of injustice, anarchy, discontent, and hatred were all around us. It seemed to me that God himself had devised, to mark my father's end, the most sustained and brutally dissonant of codas" (*Notes of a Native Son* 85).

In "Notes of a Native Son," Baldwin examined the complexity of his father's character, and their tenuous relationship. Toward the end of his life, stated Baldwin, his father found himself less in demand as a minister "and by the time he died none of his friends had come to see him for a long time. He had lived and died in an intolerable bitterness of spirit and it frightened me, as we drove home to the graveyard through those unquiet, ruined streets, to see how powerful and overflowing this bitterness could be and to realize that this bitterness was now mine" (88). Since the incident in New Jersey, Baldwin felt more connected to his father's anger and despair toward whites: "I saw that this had been for my ancestors and now would be for me an awful thing to live with and that the bitterness which had helped to kill my father could also kill me" (89). However, he also realized, although it would be difficult, that the "fight begins, however, in the heart and it now had been laid to my charge to keep my own heart free of hatred and despair" (114). This was a deep important revelation that was a foundation for his personal, political, and artistic philosophy. Although he would never be free of the fire, Baldwin had challenged himself with this difficult task— to free himself of hatred.

After his father's death, Baldwin remembered that not all of the time between them had been tumultuous. He recalled warm memories of when he was a young child, and his father had held him, grinning with pride and showing him off to others: "I had forgotten, in the rage of my growing up, how proud my father had been of me when I was little" (*Notes of a Native Son* 107).

It would take Baldwin another twelve years to write about his relationship with his father, but already, his ideas about racism and religion, and the impact of his father, began to take shape:

Baldwin's true subject, he had begun to realize even by 1943, was his difficult history, but he had not yet gained the confidence to place himself at the center of that history and treat himself as its prime representative. Much of his best writing concerns things which happened in his family, or close to it, up to the time of his father's death. But it would need a dozen or more years and the space of an ocean before these events could be persuaded to yield up the stuff of myth in essays such as "Notes of a Native Son." (Campbell 26)

Baldwin's clear and direct message conveyed his own conflicted emotions toward his father: "I had not known my father very well. We had got on badly, partly because we shared, in our different fashions, the vice of stubborn pride. When he was dead I realized that I had hardly ever spoken to him. When he was dead for a long time I began to wish I had" (86).

AT HOME IN THE VILLAGE

After his father's funeral, Baldwin quit an exhausting job at a meat-packing factory, and decided to make the break from Harlem to reside in Greenwich Village.

Baldwin also committed himself to becoming a writer—and it was not an easy path to take. This period of drifting for Baldwin was both emotionally and physically difficult. He went from one low-paying job to another, and stayed in a variety of rooms around the Village. He spent his nights wandering the Village bars, borrowing money from whoever he could, and socializing with crowds of friends and acquaintances, afraid to be alone. He spent time with Delaney, and his circle of friends widened to include numerous artists, writers, and bohemians. To a boy raised in Harlem, Greenwich Village seemed like another world:

It was seemingly the most tolerant, easygoing area in New York City. In the summer, painters displayed their pictures along Sixth Avenue and the side streets, musicians played their guitars in Washington Square Park, there were all-night coffee shops along Macdougal and Bleeker streets where you could play chess twenty-four hours a day, and in favorite bars like the Riviera, the White Horse, the Cedar Tavern and the San Remo artists of all kinds drank, argued, looked for lovers and made business contacts. (Weatherby 43)

Baldwin was one of those who spent his time at bars, talking about literature, art, and the racial divide, over liquor and cigarettes. One place in particular he liked to go to was the Calypso, a small restaurant on Macdougal Street, where he also worked for a while as a waiter. He was also beginning to write again, mostly poetry, at first, and was reading Shakespeare, Thomas Wolfe, and T.S. Eliot, expanding his views on literature and art. Soon he began to work on a novel about his father and his experience with the church called *Crying Holy*, or *In My Father's House*, which would later become *Go Tell It On the Mountain*.

Although this period of his life was exhilarating and helped shape his identity as a writer, it was also emotionally strenuous—in dealing with his father's death, facing the pressures of poverty, which seemed to constantly followed him, and experimenting with his sexuality. Baldwin had many girlfriends, and even lived with a woman for a year, but he finally decided that he was more attracted to men, which he revealed to Capouya. "I thought he was a man who had flirted with homosexuality, but I had it the wrong way around," Capouya told Weatherby (44). Others who knew Baldwin, however, were not surprised. Although most gay and lesbians were closeted in America during this time, for fear of being ostracized, losing their jobs, and being cut off from their families, in Greenwich Village, homosexuality was mostly accepted—at least on the surface. Baldwin explored the gay scene in the Village, going to bars and cruising. He had had his first homosexual experience at sixteen years old—when he developed a relationship with a man in his late thirties, a "racketeer" in Harlem, according to Weatherby (30). Although Baldwin loved him, "in a boy's way," at the time he was still preaching, and felt too conflicted by his feelings of guilt and desire. Now, however, in his twenties, he felt more confident about claiming his sexuality.

Although the Village gave the appearance of being tolerant with homosexuality and comfortable with race, Baldwin soon learned that it was not the paradise he had imagined. Although the racism was more subtle than in New Jersey, Baldwin still often felt the tension of being a black writer in a predominately white community. In the Village, only a handful of other African-Americans were part of the community, which made Baldwin feel like he stood out. This also made him more of a target. More than once, he found himself thrown out of bars, involved in shouting matches with drunken whites, or rousted by police.

His social lifestyle and lack of money made it difficult for him to find concentrated times to write, and he was beginning to doubt himself. Then at the end of the 1944, a little over a year after his father's death, Baldwin met one of his literary heroes, Richard Wright—it was a friendship that would significantly affect his artistic development. Wright's *Native Son*, published in 1940, portrayed the life of Bigger Thomas, a young black man living on the South Side of Chicago, and the social conditions that led him to commit murder and then die by the electric chair. The book sold 250,000 copies in less than six weeks, and helped bring national attention to the plight of African-Americans, exposing the devastation of poverty and racism. The novel had significantly impacted Baldwin when he first read it: "The life he described was the life I lived" (*Conversations* 223).

At thirty-six, Richard Wright, who hailed from Mississippi, was the famous and successful novelist Baldwin was hoping to become. After a mutual friend set up a meeting between the two of them, Baldwin went to Lefferts Place, Brooklyn, where Wright lived with his wife and their baby daughter. Twenty-year-old Baldwin was anxious and nervous: "It was in Brooklyn; it was winter, I was broke, naturally, shabby, hungry, and scared" (*Nobody Knows My Name* 91). He expected Wright to be terribly intimidating; however, when Wright answered the door, he greeted him with a warm smile.

Many years later, after Wright's death, Baldwin revisited this first meeting in his essay "Alas, Poor Richard:"

> We were linked together, really, because both of us were black. I had made my pilgrimage to meet him because he was the greatest black writer in the world for me.... I found expressed, for the first time in my life, the sorrow, the rage, and the murderous bitterness which was eating up my life and the lives of those around me. His work was an immense liberation and revelation for me. He became my ally and my witness, and alas! my father. (191)

Wright offered Baldwin a bourbon, and then kindly asked him what he was working on. "I was so afraid of falling of my chair and so anxious for him to be interested in me, that I told him far more about the novel that I, in fact, knew about it, madly improvising, one jump ahead of the bourbon, on all the themes which cluttered up my mind," Baldwin later recalled (192). Wright was charmed by Baldwin's intensity and passion, and he generously agreed to read the first fifty pages of his novel. Days later Wright sent the manuscript to his publishers, Harper & Brothers, who awarded Baldwin a $500 grant from the Eugene F. Saxton Memorial Trust. "He was very proud of me then," recalled Baldwin, "and I was puffed up with pleasure that he was proud, and was determined to make him prouder still" (193). Although Baldwin and Wright never gained the sort of intimate relationship that Baldwin had with Delaney, there was a type of father-son dynamic between them, which later Baldwin would rebel against.

Baldwin gave some of the grant money to his mother, and he spent the rest quickly, a habit of his that plagued him throughout his life. Harper & Brothers took an option to publish the completed novel, but Baldwin was having trouble finishing it. He labored over it intensively, working late into the night when he got home from waiting tables.

When he sent the completed version to Harper & Brothers, the novel was rejected, which was followed by a rejection by Doubleday. Baldwin felt like a failure, and he was extremely disappointed in himself. For a while, he stopped writing, and hid in shame from all of his friends: "I scarcely knew how to face anyone, let alone Richard. I was too ashamed of myself and I was sure that he was ashamed of me, too. This was utter foolishness on my part, for Richard knew far more about first novels and fledgling novelists than that; but I had been out for his approval" (*Nobody Knows My Name* 194).

Eventually, Baldwin returned to the novel, and he also began writing nonfiction. On April 12, 1947, he made his first contribution to a major journal, reviewing a book of stories by Maxim Gorki in the *Nation*. This article soon led to more published reviews and essays, and as his work circulated and he met more writers, Baldwin began to develop a reputation among New York's intelligentsia. Baldwin established relationships with the editors Sol Levitas at *The New Leader*; Philip Rahv at the *Partisan Review*; Randall Jarrell at *The Nation*; and Elliot Cohen and Robert Warshow at *Commentary*. All of these editors, notes Campbell, were white: "[I]f it was still unusual to see a black person mixing with whites in New York, it was even more surprising to find a young Negro with no formal education beyond the age of seventeen contributing regularly to the nation's top intellectual magazines" (40).

In the next year, Baldwin published his essay "The Harlem Ghetto" in *Commentary*, which was widely read and commented on for its frank discussion about race. He was still working on the novel that had been rejected, and he was also writing a book on Harlem with the artist Theodore Pelatowski. From the outside, it seemed that Baldwin was well on his way to success. However, he felt like he was headed toward a breakdown. He felt trapped—he was struggling financially, and felt the pervasive claws of racism wrapped around his throat. An editor of the *Partisan Review*, William Phillips, recalled how the issue of race seemed to be bottled up in Baldwin: "He was very articulate and he talked quite openly except for one subject—the anger inside him about being black. It took him a while to talk about being black in white society. There was some of that burning inside of him" (Weatherby 54).

Two years before, Baldwin's friend, the 24-year-old Eugene Worth, had jumped off the George Washington Bridge, plunging to his death, and his suicide haunted Baldwin—who mourned his friend, and feared he was heading in the same direction. He thought he was going to lose his mind if he stayed in New York any longer. Forty years later, he tried to explain the pressures to the *Paris Review*: "Looking for a place to live. Looking for a job. You begin to doubt your judgment, you begin to doubt everything. You become imprecise. And that's when you're beginning to go under. You've been beaten, and it's been deliberate. The whole society has decided to make you *nothing*" (234). The pain of his friends' death always stayed with him, and in his novel *Another Country*, he created a character, named Rufas Scott, who kills himself by jumping off the bridge.

Baldwin knew he needed to leave New York, but where would he go? He had never been anywhere outside of the Northeast, but he knew that many artists and writers were heading to Paris. Richard Wright, fed up with racism and government harassment, had left two years before, and even his mentor Delaney spoke of going overseas. "It wasn't so much a matter of choosing France—it was a matter of getting out of America," Baldwin later said. "I didn't know what was going to happen to me in France, but I knew what was going to happen to me in New York. If I had stayed there, I would have gone under, like my friend on the George Washington Bridge" (*Conversations* 233).

Leaving New York, however, was like an impossible dream: Baldwin had no money to buy a plane ticket and his family was in New York. Then, the proposal for the co-authored book with Pelatowski, which was never published, won a $1,500 Rosenwald Fellowship. Baldwin gave a portion of the award money to his mother, and before he spent the rest of it, he bought a one-way plane ticket to Paris. He had made up his mind—the weight of New York City was too much for him, he needed a new place to write. Tied up with guilt about deserting his family, Baldwin waited until the last day to tell them he was leaving. That afternoon, he went to Harlem to break the news. It was a difficult, emotional few hours. While his youngest sister burst into tears, Baldwin's mother was quiet. Baldwin did not know how to reassure her. Instead, he fled—and it would be almost four years before Baldwin saw her again.

AMERICAN IN PARIS

When Baldwin arrived in Paris on November 11, 1948, he was twenty-four years old. He had no grasp of the French language, and only $40 in his pocket. But he was richer in many ways—he was in Paris during a time when many American artists, novelists, and jazz musicians, including Sidney Bechet and Coleman Hawkins, were making this city their new home, creating an American colony that spent its days in cafés and salons. Although the majority of Americans were white, many black artists and writers also went to Paris, where they felt freer. Paris had a long reputation as a place where African-Americans could flourish, as seen with Josephine Baker in the 1920s. Thus, although Baldwin took a brave risk in leaving all that he knew behind, he was certainly not alone.

The day Baldwin arrived he went to Les Deux Magots, a popular café for artists and writers, where he saw Richard Wright at a crowded table. The last time Baldwin saw Wright was two years ago, right before Wright left for Paris. Wright happily greeted him: "'Hey, boy!' he cried, looking more surprised and pleased and conspiratorial than ever, and younger and happier" (*Nobody Knows My Name* 195)

Paris soon proved to be an invigorating, inspiring place to be as an artist, where neither money nor race seemed, at least at first, terribly important. At this point, Paris had not fully recovered from the effects of WWII, and many people were getting around by bike and living on food rations. However, it was possible for a foreigner to find room and board for relatively little money, and the large number of young Americans living there on the GI Bill helped build a social circle. As Paris opened Baldwin up to a world of bohemians, writers, expatriates, it also helped him to claim his identity as an American in ways he had never experienced before: "In my necessity to find the terms on which my experience could be related to that of others, Negroes and whites, writers and non-writers, I proved, to my astonishment, to be as American as any Texas G.I." (*Nobody Knows My Name* 4).

In Paris, Baldwin did not feel the oppressive race tensions he had felt in the U.S.: "I left America because I doubted my ability to survive the fury of the color problem here" (*Nobody Knows My Name* 4). In Paris, he did not need to worry about being refused service: "In America, the color of my skin had stood between myself and me; in Europe, that barrier was down" (*Notes of a Native Son* xi). As Baldwin became more comfortable in Paris, he also faced more of his deeper emotions about race that he'd been unable to admit when he was still living in New York: "What was the most difficult was the fact that I was forced to admit something I had always hidden from myself, which the American Negro has had to hide from himself as the price of his public progress; that I hated and feared white people" (*Notes of a Native Son* 7). He realized just how close he had come to becoming like his father—or like his friend, Eugene Worth. Now he had a chance to start again, to live more freely.

As Baldwin spent more time in Paris, however, he realized that the city was not free of racism. He later observed how Arab immigrants from France's colony of Algeria in northern Africa were treated as outcasts. He spent time in the Arab Quarter of the city, and in a 1973 interview, stated, "In France, the Algerian is the nigger" (*Conversations* 152).

Soon after his arrival, Baldwin's friends helped him find a room at the Hotel Verneuil, where many Left Bank bohemians were living. He quickly fell in with a group of writers and artists, who were young, gay, straight, black, and white, and rarely spent time with Wright and his crowd, which included the French existentialists, Jean-Paul Sartre and Simone de Beauvoir. Baldwin's social life in Paris resembled the one he had led in Greenwich Village. He moved freely with different crowds of people, and met other writers passing through Paris, including Saul Bellow, Truman Capote, Chester Himes, and Philip Roth, and he spent nights wandering bars and cruising. Also, similar to his days in the Village, in Paris Baldwin rarely had money. Although most of the bohemian crowd at least had some sort of income, however small, Baldwin had none. "His chaotic style of living was becoming notorious," notes Campbell. "He borrowed things and never returned them; he failed to turn up for appointments; he could not pay the rent in his own room.... he was every bit as irresponsible with other people's money as he was with his own" (57). As in Greenwich Village, much of Baldwin's time went toward socializing—drinking, staying up late with friends, eating out at restaurants were pleasures he never denied himself, even when he was broke: "I love to eat and drink—it's my melancholy conviction that I've scarcely ever had enough to eat (this is because it's impossible to eat enough if you're worried about the next meal)—and I love to argue with people who do not disagree with me too profoundly, and I love to laugh" (*Notes of a Native Son* 8). Baldwin was gregarious and generous, and always had a crowd of friends and lovers. Although Baldwin was notorious for borrowing money, showing up late, he was also irresistibly appealing and engaging. "His habits of borrowing and of not keeping appointments were not charming but the moment he was seated opposite a friend with a drink in his hand, he would become animated and humorous, intimate and brilliant—and would be forgiven" (Campbell 57).

The constant drink and cigarettes, in addition to his lack of warm clothes, contributed to Baldwin catching pneumonia during the winter of 1948–1949. He was extremely sick and bed-ridden, but the woman who owned the hotel took care of him, feeding him soup, nursing him, and forgiving his debts. Baldwin remained always grateful to her, and in his later years, when he had money to stay in better places, he occasionally went back to see her.

Baldwin was living in the city of romance, and at the turn of 1949–1950, he fell in love with Lucien Happersberger, a seventeen-year-old Swiss artist he met at a bar. Lucien was not intellectual the way most of Baldwin's friends were, but he was quick-thinking and witty, and Baldwin promptly fell for him. He was tall, slim, and good-looking, and had a gentleness to him. The two developed a close relationship that lasted to the end of Baldwin's life. The relationship went back and forth from being friends to lovers. However, Baldwin always wished for them to be lovers: "However much of a bohemian and sexual outlaw he might have seemed at times, Baldwin held on to an ideal of love," notes Campbell (61). Baldwin wanted them to share a life together—it was the most dramatic love of his life. However, Lucien didn't view their relationship in the same way: "[W]e were buddies. We accepted each other exactly as we were." Happersberger also told Campbell, "Jimmy was very romantic. He had a dream of settling down" (61). It was difficult for Baldwin not to hold onto Lucien as a lover, but even when he felt heartbroken and rejected, he supported him as a friend. For example, when Lucien came to Baldwin telling him his girlfriend was pregnant, Baldwin advised Lucien to marry her. When the baby was born, he was called "Luc-James."

In addition to the social circles and the romance, Baldwin was also trying to work on his novel, the same one he had been writing in New York. Then, in spring 1949, he received his first literary commission in Paris. Wright's friend Themistocles Hoetis, the editor of *Zero*, asked Baldwin for an essay, and Baldwin submitted "Everybody's Protest Novel," which brought him wide exposure. The essay was also published in the United States in the June 1949 *Partisan Review*, helping to further establish Baldwin on the literary scene. In "Everybody's Protest Novel," Baldwin criticizes *Uncle Tom's Cabin*, the book he once loved as a child, as a "bad novel." He argues the protest novel undermines the complexity of humanity: "But our humanity is our burden, our life; we need not battle for it; we need only to do what is infinitely more difficult—that is, accept it. The failure of the protest novel lies in its rejection of life, the human being, the denial of his beauty, dread, power, in its insistence that it is his categorization alone which is real and which cannot be transcended" (23). At the end of the essay, Baldwin turns his sights on Wright's *Native Son*—the last forty-one lines critique the protagonist, Bigger Thomas, and this part of the essay caused a stir.

The essay placed him in definitive opposition to his mentor, Richard Wright, and also irrevocably altered the relationship between them. Although they would still speak to each other, and occasionally met for drinks, they never fully patched things up. Wright felt he had been betrayed by his protégée. "Wright was furious about the *Zero* affair," Hoetis told Campbell. "He thought we'd set him up. I said we didn't set anybody up. We just got a story from the old black writer and an essay from the new. That was all there was to it. But he was very angry" (63). Baldwin, young and confident, acted surprised that Wright was angry. Later, he regretted that they could not mend their relationship, and admits he had been wrong in hurting him. In a sense, some biographers have speculated, Baldwin realized that Wright was "alas! my father" and that he needed to reject him, as he had done his own, in order to discover his own identity (191).

At this point in Baldwin's writing life, the late 19th and early 20th century American expatriate writer Henry James meant more to him than the work of Richard Wright. Baldwin felt that Wright was mostly concerned with political and social agendas, whereas in James's greatest novels, such as *The Portrait of a Lady*, *The Wings of the Dove*, and *The Golden Bowl*, political and social issues are absent. James was more interested in perception and psychology than in plot, which appealed to Baldwin's artistic sensibilities. Another writer who influenced him during this time was the white Southern writer, William Faulkner.

Baldwin's nonfiction publications helped build his reputation as an important writer, but he was still struggling with his first novel, and was becoming frustrated by not being able to complete it. He had been working on the novel for ten years, and by the fall of 1951, Baldwin fell into a depression.

> Moving from one cold, cramped hotel to another, with little privacy and less money, Baldwin found it hard to settle down to his novel. Paris was great for living, great for talking, which was one of Baldwin's true skills, but less good for working. The problem was the pleasure. Left Bank society was mainly café society, and, flitting easily from one hand-out to another, Baldwin, if he happened to be without Lucien, could always be sure of finding company, and if he was without money, of finding a ready hand to buy him a drink. (Campbell 72)

Baldwin knew if he was ever going to finish this novel, he needed to get away from Paris, just as before, he had needed to leave Greenwich Village.

At the end of 1951, Baldwin went with Lucien to his parents' chalet in the mountains of Switzerland, in a village, Loeche-es-Bains, about four hours from Milan. Baldwin had never seen a landscape such as this, with the snow-covered mountains, and similarly, the Swiss inhabitants had never seen a black man before, which often caused a strange tension. In his essay "Stranger in the Village" Baldwin wrote about the villagers touching his hair, or rubbing his skin in awe: "But I remain as much a stranger today as I was the first day I arrived and the children shout *Neger! Neger* as I walk along the streets," he wrote (161). He added, "I knew that they did not mean to be unkind, and I know it now ... The children who shout Neger! have no way of knowing the echoes this sound raises in me" (162).

Despite this troubling experience, and the potential rage and humiliation these scenes stirred up, the isolation of the setting fueled Baldwin. For three months, Baldwin worked on the novel, listening to Bessie Smith records: "It was Bessie Smith, through her tone and her cadence, who helped me to dig back to the way I myself must have spoken when I was a pickaninny, and to remember the things I had heard and seen and felt" (*Nobody Knows My Name* 5).

Baldwin sent off *Go Tell It On the Mountain* to his agent Helen Strauss in New York, and several weeks later, he heard from the reputable publishing house Alfred A. Knopf. The editors expressed interest in the novel and wanted to meet him. Could he come to New York?

Finally, the novel would be published. But, again, there was the problem of money. How could he go back to America when he didn't have a cent? Fortunately, his actor friend Marlon Brando, who he had met in the Village years before, was visiting Paris and loaned Baldwin the $500 to buy a ticket on the next ship going back to New York.

When Baldwin arrived to America, his brother David, who he was closest to, was waiting for him at the dock. It had been three and half years since Baldwin had last seen his family, and although he felt happy to see them, he still wrestled with the old guilt for deserting them. While he was living the life of a bohemian overseas, his family was still living in a squalid apartment building and his mother was cleaning white people's houses. He wanted to make his mother proud, hoping one day he could care for her the way she had for him.

To Baldwin's disappointment, Knopf was not ready to publish his novel—first they wanted revisions—and offered him little money. They gave him $250, and promised another $750 after the revisions were completed. Baldwin followed through with most of the editorial suggestions, but he felt in general that the editors did not fully understand the book. He delivered the completed manuscript to Knopf in July, and was relieved to be finished with it. He had been in the United States long enough. Although he was happy to see his family and old friends, he felt the atmosphere to be stifling—this was the period of McCarthyism and communist witch-hunting, and many of his writer and artist friends seemed too scared to talk openly about politics. So Baldwin gave part of his advance to his family, and used the rest to book his passage back to France.

FINDING HIS WAY HOME

Go Tell It on the Mountain was published in May 1953, and Baldwin, who had struggled for ten years to complete the book, could hardly contain his excitement. He was even more thrilled when the book met critical success, with outstanding reviews in the *New York Times*, *London's Times*, *Saturday Review*, and the *Sun-Times*.

However, the thrill of success did not last long. The advance from Knopf soon disappeared, and with it, Baldwin's high spirits also dissipated. By the fall, he was depressed again, unable to write and feeling oppressed by poverty. Although ideas came to him quickly, they disappeared just as fast. Baldwin often had difficulty following through with something, and because he moved around frequently, he rarely found concentrated blocks of time in which to write. He was also troubled by his relationship with Lucien. The two were close, but Baldwin wanted more: "The same two obsessions dominated Baldwin throughout every period, in every place: his love life and his writing life," attests Campbell. "Both tended towards a state of anarchy" (85). One highlight in 1953 was that his mentor and good friend Beauford Delaney arrived in Paris, which lifted Baldwin's mood for a short period. He then won a Guggenheim fellowship, which provided him with enough money to return to the United States. This time, Lucien went with him.

Baldwin arrived in New York in early June, 1954. He and Lucien lived together on Greenwich Street, but again, Baldwin found little time to write. Baldwin's moods rose and fell, and trouble ensued with Lucien.

According to Campbell, "He was obsessed with the idea of a happy, settled domestic life with Lucien. Even if Lucien had been available and agreeable—and he was neither: he was married and as domesticated as he ever wanted to be—Baldwin would have most likely have grown restless anyway before long" (95).

Then in August, Baldwin had the opportunity to attend the MacDowell Colony, an artist and writer's residency in New Hampshire, where he found the peace and quiet he needed to concentrate on his work, without worrying about his love life or his struggles with money.

Baldwin completed his novel *Giovanni's Room*. He also had the opportunity to have his play, *Amen Corner*, about a character based on Mother Horn, performed at Howard University in May 1955. Although the play would not be produced on Broadway for another ten years, the student production, headed by the African-American poet, playwright, and teacher Owen Dodson, pleased Baldwin. He enjoyed working with the college students and spending time at the university.

During this time, Baldwin was also working on an essay on his father after his old high school classmate, Sol Stein, suggested he publish a collection of essays. The essay turned into "Notes of a Native Son," viewed by many as one of Baldwin's most moving and eloquent pieces of writing in his lifetime. The essay is a courageous reconciliation with his father, as well as a rejection of his father's hatred—and it is a graceful, thoughtful piece of writing that captures Baldwin's process in understanding his father's life. When the book was published by Beacon Press in late 1955, it was an immediate success and instantly recognized as a small classic. One of the most important reviews of praise came from the famous African-American poet Langston Hughes, who had been critical of *Go Tell It On The Mountain*.

However, Baldwin did not find similar success with his recently completed novel, *Giovanni's Room*. His agent Helen Strauss expressed disappointment and even, according to Campbell, advised Baldwin "to burn it." When, against her judgment, she sent the novel to Knopf, the editors rejected the book on the grounds that it was too controversial. Baldwin had surprised his publishers by writing a novel that contained no black characters—and shocked them by writing candidly about a love affair between two men. In this era, most gay men and lesbians stayed in the closet, and the editors at Knopf were too nervous to risk publishing something that was still quite taboo. Baldwin was furious by the rejection. In many ways, Baldwin was ahead of his time. He was open about his sexuality, but rejected labels; he believed in love—regardless of gender. He once said, "Well, now we've really, you know, we've walked into very marshy ground because those terms, homosexual, bisexual, heterosexual are 20th-century terms which, for me, really have very little meaning. I've never, myself, in watching myself and watching other people, watching life, been able to discern exactly where the barriers were. Life being what life is, passion being what passion is" (*Conversations* 54–55).

Baldwin refused to abandon this novel, even if he had to go across the ocean to find an audience. He felt exhausted and disappointed in general by New York, and the rejection only intensified his feelings. In the fall of 1955, Baldwin sailed again for France. This time, Lucien did not go with him. Instead, Baldwin's new lover, Arnold, a musician from Harlem, was his traveling companion.

In Europe, Baldwin found a more open-minded response to his novel. Michael Joseph, a small London publishing house, was more than willing to publish *Giovanni's Room*. The publishers bought the novel for $4,000 and promised to publish whatever else Baldwin wrote. Then, in America, Dial Press also published the novel and remained Baldwin's publishers for over twenty years.

Giovanni's Room is told from the perspective of a white American living in Paris, who falls in love with a man named Giovanni, but in the end, betrays him. "Giovanni's Room was among the first American novels to treat the subject of homosexuality with the same frankness permitted for discussions of heterosexual love," asserted Campbell (102). It was courageous for Baldwin to write and to publish this novel at a time when homosexuality was illegal on both sides of the Atlantic. Despite the conservative atmosphere, once the book was published, it received great acclaim.

Still, even with this success, Baldwin could not shake off his unhappiness and loneliness. He had many transient love affairs, and spent his evenings with friends, drinking and arguing. His expressive eyes, flashing with intensity, drew people in, as did his warm smile and congenial nature. The writer Norman Mailer recalled how personable Baldwin was, how people were drawn to him: "Jimmy had an absolutely wonderful personality in those years," he said. "I don't think there was anyone in the literary world who was more beloved than Jimmy. He had the loveliest manners. And he had these extraordinary moods: he walked around with a deep mahogany melancholy when he was unhappy, and when things amused him it was wonderful to watch him laugh, because it came out of this sorrow he had" (Campbell 140). These mood swings, however, were difficult for Baldwin to balance, and although he had many friends, loneliness ate at him. Baldwin described himself during these years as "a very tight, tense, lean, abnormally ambitious," young man trying to find his way:

> I wandered through Paris, the underside of Paris, drinking, screwing, fighting—it's a wonder I wasn't killed. And then it was morning, I would somehow be home—usually, anyway— and the typewriter would be there, staring at me; and the manuscript of the new novel, which it seemed I would never be able to achieve, and from which clearly I was never going to be released, was scattered all over the floor. (*Nobody Knows My Name* 224)

Baldwin, now thirty-two years old, had three published books, which helped him win a grant from the National Institute of Arts and Letters in 1956. He was already building a successful writing career, yet still he struggled with his own confidence, fearing the "staring" typewriter. Furthermore, although in America his literary reputation was growing, he was not always recognized in Parisian literary circles. He began to consider returning to the United States—but not only for his career. Something else, much more profound and frightening, tugged at him.

In the United States, after the Supreme Court ruling against segregated education in 1954 in *Brown* v. *the Board of Education*, violent confrontations rippled across the South. When a woman named Rosa Parks refused to give up her seat on a bus to a white man in Montgomery, Alabama, she set off a boycott of the buses by African-Americans that lasted eleven months and resulted in victory in 1956. The boycott was led by a young, fiery preacher named Dr. Martin Luther King, Jr., who was just beginning to become a national figure.

As racial tensions worsened, the Civil Rights Movement was building. Baldwin felt disconnected from the movement, and guilty for living so freely in France. While others were laying their lives on the line, he was spending his time in cafés. Although he felt drawn to this activism, he was afraid to return to the United States. He contributed to the discussion on Civil Rights in ways that he could, from afar, with his writing. For example, he published an essay on Faulkner for the *Partisan Review*, in which he criticized William Faulkner for his advice to blacks to "go slow," but Baldwin knew this was not enough. As tension increased in the United States, Baldwin's conflicting feelings deepened. He realized that in order to contribute to the Civil Rights Movement, he needed to be living in the United States, but a big part of him wanted to remain in Paris, where he felt safe.

In September, 1956, Baldwin's rocky relationship with his lover Arnold ended, and Baldwin went to Corsica for a Conference of Negro-African Writers & Artists, in which Richard Wright was one of the speakers. The conference left little impact on Baldwin, except for the fact that W.E.B. Dubois, one of the speakers, never showed up because the United States had denied him a passport. This incident was another reminder to Baldwin that the political atmosphere in the United States was growing more explosive and dangerous. Still, Baldwin made no concrete plans to return.

Then, one day he came across a newsstand in Paris, and on the front page was a picture of fifteen-year-old girl in Charlotte, North Carolina. As she tried to walk up the steps to school, a violent white mob barricaded her from reaching door. According to Campbell, "It took almost a year for him to act, but it was on that bright September afternoon in 1956 that the image of a young girl being jeered and spat at had implanted in his conscience the knowledge that, whether he wanted to or not, he must go home," (112). As Baldwin heard more news about the United States, he knew he could not bury his head, as he explained in an interview fifteen years later: "I got tired and I began to be ashamed, sitting in cafés in Paris and explaining Little Rock and Tennessee. I thought it was easier to go home" (*Conversations* 84).

VIEW OF THE SOUTH

If Baldwin's fundamental subject was himself and America, then he had to return to the United States, where African-Americans were engaged in a revolution that would profoundly alter American society. Baldwin returned in July 1957 to an America that was exploding—

especially in the South. In 1954, in *Brown* v. *Board of Education*, the Supreme Court deemed segregation illegal; however, states in the south refused to recognize this ruling. Every day, in Little Rock, Arkansas; Birmingham, Alabama; Atlanta, Georgia; and Charlotte, North Carolina, African-Americans—including schoolchildren—were being beaten and threatened with death, over the right to attend the same schools as white children. Civil Rights leaders were being targeted, with bricks flying through their windows at night and their children threatened. White supremacist groups—the Ku Klux Klan the newly formed White Citizens' Councils—increased their violence and opposition to desegregation.

Baldwin was terrified of the South, but he believed that, in order to understand the depth the Civil Rights Movement, he needed to go there. Since he was a child, listening to his grandmother and father's stories about slavery, lynching, and endless violence, he had always been terrified of the South. But he decided to face his fears. He landed a commission from *Harper's* magazine, and for the first time in his life, Baldwin traveled to the South: "I was past thirty, and I had never seen this land before" (*Nobody Knows My Name* 99). First, Baldwin went to Charlotte, North Carolina, where he met with several black children who had been threatened, stoned, and spat on for trying to integrate formerly white schools, which he chronicles in his essay "Nobody Knows My Name." He explains that their parents sent them to attend these schools "because they want the child to receive the education which will allow him to defeat, possibly escape, and not impossibly help one day abolish the stifling environment in which they see, daily, so many children perish" (104). Then he went to Atlanta, Georgia, where he met Civil Right's leader Martin Luther King for the first time. King's intelligence and charisma impressed Baldwin, and he was drawn to his message of nonviolence and love.

On this trip, Baldwin also went to Alabama, where heard King preach, and Little Rock. Although he often felt like an outsider, explaining that the African American from the north "who finds himself in the South is in a position similar to that of the son of the Italian emigrant who finds himself in Italy ... Both are in countries they have never seen, but which they cannot fail to recognize" (*Nobody Knows My Name* 98), he also felt a deep connection to the land. In "Nobody Knows

My Name," he described the powerful feelings of seeing the red-earth of Georgia from the plane:

> I pressed my face against the window, watching the earth come closer; soon we were just above the tops of trees. I could not suppress the thought that this earth had acquired its color from the blood that had dripped down from these trees. My mind was filled with the image of a black man, younger than I, perhaps, or my own age, hanging from a tree, while white men watched him and cut his sex from him with a knife. (100)

In a sense, this trip also connected him to his dead father, realizing that "he must have seen such sights ... or heard of them, or had this danger touch him" (100). Baldwin, his fear stirred up, met with African-American students who were being harassed and threatened for wanting to attend a school, the children's parents, and a variety of others, including a white principal. He talked to many people and absorbed everything. One person who made a profound impression on him was an old man he observed on a segregated bus: "his eyes seemed to say that what I was feeling he had been fleeing, at much higher pressure, all his life. But my eyes would never see the hell his eyes had seen" (110).

When Baldwin left the South, he knew he would never forget what he'd seen. This trip left him a changed person—his life would never be the same. He felt unequivocally committed to the Civil Rights Movement. But when he arrived back to New York, he was physically and emotionally exhausted. Although he felt pulled to be a more active part of the movement, he also knew that he could not abandon his writing—this was who he was.

At this time, Baldwin was writing for the *New York Times*, *Harper's*, *Esquire*, and *The New Yorker*, a prestigious position that no other black writer filled. Baldwin was, in a sense, one of the most cosmopolitan writers of his day.

He returned to the MacDowell Colony to work on a dramatization of *Giovanni's Room*, and in the spring of 1958, the Actor's Studio presented the play as a workshop production, with Baldwin's Turkish friend Engin Cezzar in the leading role. Although the workshop did not materialize into a full-scale production, working in theater excited

Baldwin, and planted in him a seed to be more involved. For a while, he also became the director Elia Kazan's assistant on two new Broadway plays, including Tennessee Williams's *Sweet Bird of Youth*.

Although the people he encountered in the South would never leave his mind, New York felt far away from what he had witnessed. In the late 1950s New York sparkled with the energy of artists, musicians, and writers, with talk of modern jazz, method acting, the *Village Voice*, and the Beats. Baldwin was a part of this energy. He continued his life of excessive socializing and drinking, doing most of his writing after midnight and sleeping past noon.

Baldwin bought a small apartment at 81 Horatio Street, in Greenwich Village, with a view of Hudson River, where he entertained numerous guests and threw himself into several writing projects. He was working on a novel, short stories, and essays.

In 1959, the publication of "The Discovery of What it Means to be American" and "Nobody Knows My Name" helped to establish Baldwin as a important commentator on racial conditions in America. Then, in February 1959, Baldwin won a fellowship from the Ford Foundation for $12,000 over a four-year period for his novel-in-progress *Another Country*. He left the United States again for France.

FINDING A BALANCE

As Baldwin achieved more fame, Paris was becoming like New York—he found it more difficult to find the privacy he needed in order to write. He was a celebrity writer, expanding his long list of well-known friends, which included Nina Simone, Paule Marshall, Nikki Giovanni, Norman Mailer, Marlon Brando, William Styron, and Lorraine Hansberry, the author of the play *A Raisin in the Sun*. Baldwin traveled often, and on his travels, he also met and interviewed the Swiss director Ingmar Bergman and the actor Charlie Chaplin for *Esquire* magazine.

Balancing his need for privacy with his need to be around people was always a delicate matter for Baldwin. "I was trembling on the edge of great revelations, was being prepared for a very long journey, and might now begin, having survived my apprenticeship (but had I survived it?) a great work. I might really become a great writer," he explained. "But in order to do this I would have to sit down at the typewriter again, alone—I would have to accept my despair" (*Nobody Knows My Name* 223).

Although he craved isolation, being alone was often difficult. His friend, the actor and singer Harry Belafonte, told Weatherby, "[Baldwin] was very vulnerable personally. I have met few people quite as tortured as Jimmy. I mean personally. In public he didn't show it. He was quite outspoken, he didn't hide his feelings about most things" (142).

Back in New York again, Baldwin's time was even more splintered, as he tried to find time to work on his novel *Another Country*, socialize with friends, spend time with his family, and become more active in the Civil Rights Movement. He began delivering lectures at colleges, quickly developing a reputation as a brilliant, fiery speaker, perhaps remnant of his young preacher days. His enthusiastic connection to students was palpable. His friend Dr. Kenneth Clark recalled:

> He gave many, many talks to students and other groups. He impressed me as resembling an Old Testament prophet. For a while I was afraid that his total involvement in meetings with large and small groups would interfere with his writing. I saw him fluctuating between hope and despair. At times he would call and ask if we could meet so that he could spew out this anguish. He was concerned about the future of America. He saw a lack of concern or an inability in his nation to deal ethically with the problem of race. (Weatherby 140)

In his lectures, Baldwin spoke about American racism and American identity, subjects which he was becoming more and more passionate about. His ideas deepened, grew more profound and complex. "Whether I like it or not, or whether you like it or not, we are bound together forever. We are part of each other. What is happening to every Negro in this country at any time is also happening to you. There is no way around this," he proclaimed in "In Search of a Majority" (136). Although Baldwin was depressed and horrified at America's treatment of African Americans, he believed people must unite, not separate, in order for there to be hope for the future: "I think that what we really have to do is to create a country in which there are no minorities—for the first time in the history of the world. The one thing that all Americans have in common is that they have no other identity apart from the identity which is being achieved on this continent" (137). Baldwin believed Americans could save their country: "Now, this country is going to be transformed. It will not be transformed by an act of God, but by all of us, by you and me. I don't believe any longer that we can afford to say that is entirely out of our hands. We made the world we're living in and we have to make it over" (*Nobody Knows My Name* 154). According to Weatherby, Baldwin "spoke brilliantly, always gracious with questioners, but quite uncompromising, never defensive nor apologetic. His theme was that it wasn't a question of whether whites would accept blacks but whether blacks could forgive whites" (Weatherby 162).

Baldwin was in a unique position of addressing the problems of racism to a mostly white audience. For all his life, even with the more radical views he held in his later years, Baldwin had both black and white friends. He spent time meeting with members of Student Nonviolent Coordinating Committee (SNCC), the NAACP, and the Southern Christian Leadership Council (SCLC), and in the years to come, would become friendly with a range of black activists, including Malcolm X and Huey Long. Yet, during his life, he was also friends with such unlikely figures as the writer Norman Mailer, who was known as radical, rebellious young writer in the New York scene.

Norman Mailer was the well-known author of *The Naked and the Dead* as well as several other novels, and he had also written a long essay "The White Negro" about the hipsters of the Beat Generation. Although Baldwin's general view of beatniks was that their hipness and their cool were artificial, he was fond of Mailer, recalling their first meeting in his essay "The Black Boy Looks at the White Boy," in which "the toughest kid on the block was meeting the toughest kid on the block" (218). In Paris in the fifties, when Mailer was there with his wife, they had grown close; however, their friendship grew more strained by the sixties, partly due to Mailer's *Advertisement for Myself*, in which he criticized other writers, including Baldwin. Baldwin recalled reading passages aloud with his friends, the writers William Styron and James Jones. Baldwin was stung by Mailer's description that he was "too charming to be a writer" and his writing was "sprayed with perfume" (Weatherby 165). "But the condescension infuriated me; also, to tell the truth, my feelings were hurt," Baldwin wrote in "The Black Boy" (234).

Baldwin's list of famous writer and artist friends continued to grow, but no one impacted him as Richard Wright had. In November, 1960,

Baldwin received the news that Richard Wright was dead at age fifty-four. Baldwin's complex feelings of guilt and admiration, as well as his criticism, culminated in his essay, "Alas, Poor Richard," in which he decided that "Richard Wright was never, really, the social and polemical writer he took himself to be" (184). Baldwin's honest grief, "the man I fought so hard and who meant so much to me, is gone," is complicated by the fact that, "We might have been friends, for example, but I cannot honestly say that we were" (189). In this essay, Baldwin returns to the source of his conflict with Wright, and admits now that perhaps he had been too brash with "Everybody's Protest Novel:" "What made it most painful was that Richard was right to be hurt, I was wrong to have hurt him. He saw clearly enough, far more clearly than I had dared to allow myself to see, what I had done: I had used his work as a kind of springboard into my own" (197). Baldwin also wonders that if part of the trouble between them, in addition to their twenty year age difference, stemmed from the fact that Baldwin had never seen the south, Wright's homeland. Despite their different experiences and perspectives, Baldwin felt close to Wright and wished they would have reconciled, "for it would have been nothing less than that so universally desired, so rarely achieved reconciliation between spiritual father and spiritual son" (201). Unfortunately, the split between never healed, and, "This was a great loss for me" (202).

THE WITNESS

When Baldwin's collection of essays *Nobody Knows My Name* was published in 1961, it went straight to the bestseller list, where it remained for six months. The enthusiastic reviews and high quantity of sales helped boost Baldwin's fame and status outside of the literary world, and helped make him the best-known and most important black writer in America. People looked to him as an authority on race relations in America. Throughout the diverse thirteen essays runs a common thread: that blacks and whites are tied together by history, and that the future of the country depends on the connection between them. As the Civil Rights Movement continued to grow, Baldwin's fire augmented, his interviews and speeches exhibiting "an authority and a depth of conviction (and also an anger) which is new, which was not present in the letters home from Paris just five years before" (Campbell 145).

Speaking engagements, fund raisers, and interviews quickly swallowed his time, and with all of this media attention, his social life also expanded—with more lovers and sycophants, more parties and dinners to attend. Despite all the action, Baldwin managed to complete an impressive amount of work in the late 1950s and early 1960s. Yet he also knew that if he did not settle down with *Another Country*, in isolation, he would never finish the novel.

In 1962, Baldwin left America again, in hopes to explore his roots in Africa. *The New Yorker* had given him an advance to write an article about the experience; however, instead of ending up in Africa, Baldwin went to Turkey. "We gave him an advance," said the editor William Shawn, "and then we didn't hear from him again. For years" (Campbell 153). In Istanbul, Baldwin stayed with his friend Cezzar, rested happily, and completed his novel *Another Country*, which he had been working on for six years.

To celebrate the publication, Dial Press threw a lavish party in New York, with family, friends and celebrities in attendance. *Another Country* brought in mostly positive reviews, and also achieved mainstream success; when it was reissued in paperback in 1963, it was the second-largest-selling book of the year (after William Golding's *Lord of the Flies*). The novel, which includes bisexual and interracial relationships and explicit sexual scenes, also inspired cries of obscenity in the South, and the book was banned in New Orleans, Louisiana. But overall, Baldwin was happy with the novel and the critical response: "I think *Another Country* is my best novel so far. Not because I achieved everything I wanted to in it—in that respect, I'm only at the beginning of my life as a writer. But *Another Country* was harder and more challenging than anything I'd ever attempted, and I didn't cheat in it" (*Conversations* 34).

Baldwin eventually reached Africa, a year after setting out. He went with his sister Gloria, and for two months they traveled through Senegal, Ghana, and Sierra Leone. Baldwin enjoyed himself, but experienced no revelation about coming back to his African roots. However, he still felt he was not ready to write the article. Instead, he decided to give *The New Yorker* the essay on Black Muslims that he had been working on for *Commentary*.

For some time, Baldwin had been making notes for a long personal essay that spanned his days as a Young Minister to the development of the Civil Rights Movement, but he was having trouble pulling it together. Then Norman Podhoretz, the editor at *Commentary*, suggested that Baldwin also write about the Black Muslims, in order to link the essay to the present. So before the Africa trip, in the summer of 1961, Baldwin had traveled to Chicago to meet the Honorable Elijah Muhammad, the leader of the Nation of Islam.

Although most Americans regarded Martin Luther King as the principal black leader, his homeland was in the South. As increasing tension grew in the north, in Detroit, Chicago, and Philadelphia, with ghettos being overrun by crime, drug addiction, and poverty, it was Elijah Muhammad, not King, who found support. The Nation of Islam, its followers known as Black Muslims, believed in a black separatist movement—opposite from Martin Luther King's hope for peaceful integration. The chief lieutenant was Malcolm X, a brilliant speaker and leader, and its founder was Honorable Elijah Muhammad, who as a boy had watched white men lynch his father.

Although Baldwin was a committed integrationist and a devoted admirer of King's, he also believed that King had little command in the North and did not understand its cities. When he was introduced to Muhammad at his mansion on Chicago's South Side, Baldwin felt immediately drawn to him, as he was years ago to Mother Horn: "The central quality in Elijah's face is pain, and his smile is a witness to it— pain so old and deep and black that it becomes personal and particular only when he smiles" (*The Fire Next Time* 64). He also felt unnerved by his presence: "He made me think of my father and me as we might have been if we had been friends" (64).

Despite Elijah's allure, he did not convince Baldwin of his separatist beliefs. His description of whites as "devils" perhaps caused Baldwin to remember his father's anger—how the bitterness destroyed his life. Although Baldwin admired the Black Muslims' pride and dignity, and admitted there was some truth in the idea of fighting back, Baldwin believed the core message was simplistic, that blacks could never be separate from America, and also, that separatism was inherently racist. Since he was a young boy, Baldwin had surrounded himself with both black and white friends, much to his father's disappointment, and in fact, after his dinner at the mansion, he was headed to spend time with white friends at a bar downtown. Baldwin realized that he was in the middle, a position that in later years would provide him a target for both blacks and whites, and according to Weatherby, "there were times when he wavered and wondered if he had made the right decision" (201). However, the negative memories of his father's bitterness and hatred were more powerful than any utopian ideas of separation, and Baldwin believed that in order to heal as a nation and to achieve a more meaningful identity, blacks and whites deeply needed each other.

When Baldwin finished the long personal essay, instead of sending it to *Commentary*, as he had promised, Baldwin sold it to *The New Yorker*. For the 20,000 words of "Down at the Cross," Baldwin received $6,500 from *The New Yorker*, nearly twice the annual income of the average Harlem family in 1962. Baldwin's behavior was considered irresponsible and unprofessional. The editors of *Commentary*, understandably, felt betrayed and angry, and he never wrote for the magazine again.

The editors at *The New Yorker*, on the other hand, were delighted. "I would say that it was one of only two or three things that really caused a sensation during my time at the magazine," the editor William Shawn told Campbell. "*The New Yorker* came out week after week, and normally there was a consistent excellence about the writing. But Baldwin's piece had a political content. It was exciting. It was unexpected. If you read it now, the ideas might seem like generally assumed ideas—but then he was saying things that hadn't been said before. And everybody was talking about it" (160). The essay, published in the November 17, 1962, issue, became the talk of the town, and the magazine's sales soared.

In "Down at the Cross," Baldwin weaves together his experience in the church as a child, as well as his meeting with Elijah:

> It was very strange to stand with Elijah for those few moments, facing those vivid, violent, so problematical streets. I felt very close to him, and really wished to be able to love and honor him as a witness, an ally, and a father. I felt that I knew something of his pain and his fury, and yes, even his beauty. Yet precisely because of the reality and the nature of those streets—because of what he conceived as his responsibility and what I took to be mine—we would always be strangers, and possibly, one day, enemies. (78)

Baldwin's hope for the future outweighed pessimism: "I know that people can be better than they are. We are capable of bearing a great burden, once we discover that the burden is reality and arrive where reality is" (91).

Although Baldwin admits in his essay that the idea of integration is sometimes baffling, "Do I really *want* to be integrated into a burning house?" (*The Fire Next Time* 94), he reaches the conclusion that in order to save the future of the country, blacks and whites must profoundly realize their connection. He warns white Americans about the dire consequences of not addressing the racial problem, prophesying an apocalypse if Americans did not change: Americans must come to terms with their past and create a society without segregation and separation, a society based on deep and profound love.

"It was a visionary sermon; Baldwin had taken on the role of confessor to the American people," explains Campbell (161). One week later, Baldwin graced the cover of *Time*, and requests for interviews poured in, as did invitations for parties, fundraisers, and rallies. *Time* described Baldwin as a nervous, slight, almost fragile figure, filled with frets and fears.

> He is effeminate in manner, drinks considerably, smokes cigarettes in chains, and he often loses his audience with overblown arguments. Nevertheless, in the U.S. today there is not another writer, white or black, who expresses with such poignancy and abrasiveness the dark realities of the racial ferment in North and South. (Weatherby 205)

After the publication in *The New Yorker*, Dial Press published the essay, along with another short one called "My Dungeon Shook" as *The Fire Next Time*. The editor at Dial Press, James Silberman, stated that with the publication of this book, critics began to view Baldwin as an essayist not a novelist. "It was very influential. It altered people's views of his literary talent ... It was a very sophisticated black man's warning to the white world" (Weatherby 206). Baldwin received $65,000 for *The Fire Next Time*, which stayed in the top five on the non-fiction bestseller lists for forty-one weeks and won the George Polk Memorial Award for outstanding magazine reporting.

America was turning to Baldwin to hear what he had to say on Civil Rights, on the future of America, and on black and white relations, and Baldwin continued to fulfill this role as writer, spokesman, and celebrity. In 1962, he went to Mississippi to meet and support James Meredith, the only black student enrolled in the previously all-white college, the University of Mississippi. Because of the threats and violence, President Kennedy had sent in 20,000 federal troops to protect Meredith and keep the peace. Baldwin also met Medgar Evers, the NAACP's chief representative in Mississippi, and accompanied him in investigating a murder in rural Mississippi.

The crisis at the University of Mississippi had shocked the Kennedy administration, which was only beginning to realize how deeply the South was entrenched in ideas of white superiority. After the violence in Mississippi, President Kennedy proposed a Civil Rights Bill to Congress, and although Civil Rights leaders were hopeful about the administration, they also felt much more needed to be accomplished. Frustration and tension throughout the country increased, and in May 1963, the American public was outraged when the police in Birmingham, Alabama blasted black children, who were peacefully protesting segregation, with water from high-pressure fire hoses and unleashed attack dogs on them.

After this incident, Attorney General Robert Kennedy, the president's brother, attempted to reach out to the Civil Rights leaders. He invited Baldwin to his Virginia home, but Baldwin, in typical manner, showed up late, and Kennedy needed to fly out that afternoon. So Kennedy suggested they meet in New York, with a group of leading African-Americans to be assembled by Baldwin. Baldwin invited a wide range of prominent Civil Rights activists: Lena Horne, singer and actress; Harry Belafonte, singer and actor; the white actor Rip Torn; Lorraine Hansberry, playwright; Clarence Jones, who was one of Martin Luther King's lawyers; Edwin Berry, director of the Chicago Urban League; Kenneth Clark, educator and psychologist; Baldwin's brother David; and Jerome Smith, a young black activist and Freedom Rider who'd been beaten terribly in Mississippi. Although King had been invited, he was unable to attend on such short notice, and asked Clark to represent him. Kennedy brought Burke Marshall, one of his top aides, for the meeting.

The groups met on May 24, 1963, both with high hopes. However, from the beginning, the meeting was filled with tension. Kennedy apparently had expected a somber discussion, with perhaps a simple solution, and he was not prepared for the emotional, furious outpouring. The meeting quickly turned into a heated confrontation, with Baldwin's group wanting to impress upon Kennedy what it felt like to be black in America—they wanted him to grasp the fear, frustration, and anger. When Jerome Smith, who still had visible welts from the beating in the South, told Kennedy he was on the verge of picking up a gun, the meeting fell apart, as Kennedy interpreted Smith's remark as a personal attack. Smith went on to say that he would never fight for his country, which appalled Kennedy. He criticized Smith for his lack of patriotism, failing to see the truth of how blacks felt—that they were not being protected and supported by their own government. To Baldwin and the others, Kennedy's shock and dismissal only reinforced their fear that the Kennedy administration, as well as much of white America, was out of touch with the reality of racism and segregation. After the meeting broke up out of sheer exhaustion, both parities felt more frustrated and distrustful than before.

Notably, after this meeting, the FBI began to take serious interest in Baldwin, whose name had first come to their attention in 1960, with his brief flirtation with the Fair Play for Cuba Committee (FPCC). The FBI had a long list of people it was watching, including Wright before his death, and Martin Luther King. Baldwin went under FBI surveillance because of his "subversive statements" and his homosexuality. By the time Baldwin's file was closed in 1974, it was comprised of 1,750 pages.

The Civil Rights Movement continued to gain power, and on June 11, President Kennedy addressed the nation on radio and TV about civil rights—and yet the violence continued. The same night Kennedy went on the air, the NAACP leader Medgar Evers was assassinated in Jackson, Mississippi. But black Americans refused to be silenced by the violence. At the height of the Civil Rights Movement, on August 28, 1963, Martin Luther King led a quarter of a million people on the March on Washington, in which he delivered his famous "I Have a Dream" speech. Baldwin was thrilled with the impact of the march, but he was disappointed that he'd been excluded from King's list of speakers; most likely, biographers concur, he was excluded because of his homosexuality. Still, that summer, the mood of the Civil Rights Movement was optimistic and hopeful. Then two and a half weeks after the March, the Sixteenth Street Baptists Church in Birmingham was bombed and four young black girls were killed.

Baldwin was on a speaking-tour when he received the news of the

Birmingham bombing. It first stunned him, then accelerated his protest activity. The tragedy also marked a further weakening of his unquestioning support of King's policy of non-violent resistance.

On October 9, 1963, Baldwin went with his brother David to help launch the SNCC's voter-registration drive in Selma, Alabama. Baldwin was stunned by what he witnessed. Applicants were lined up outside the courthouse, intending to claim their legal right to vote, and the intimidation by the police began almost immediately. No one who left the line could return to it, and when Baldwin and his brother attempted to give the exhausted people refreshments, they were stopped by police. Crowds of people stood in the sweltering heat, but at the end of the day, only about 20–50 people were admitted into the courthouse. Violence continued to spread across American, and on November 22, 1963, the assassination of President Kennedy left an already tense nation devastated.

The End of a Movement

The mood of the Civil Rights Movement was changing; in some parts of the country, Malcolm X was as popular as King. Baldwin threw himself into the fray. He burned with fire, and his speeches impressed people—he was mesmerizing, fiery, and speaking mostly to well-educated whites. Baldwin still believed there was hope to change America. "I'm forced to be an optimist; I'm forced to believe that we can survive whatever we must survive, but the future of the Negro in this country is precisely as bright or as dark as the future of the country," he said in 1965. "It is entirely up to the American people whether or not they are going to face and deal with and embrace the stranger whom they maligned so long" (*Conversations* 45).

What time Baldwin could find for writing at this point he gave mostly to a play *Blues for Mister Charlie*, which was based on the 1955 lynching of fourteen-year-old Emmett Till in Mississippi. Between the spring of 1963 and the spring of 1964, Baldwin only published five articles, all which were the texts of speeches. The physical and emotional energy demanded by the Civil Rights campaign made it difficult for Baldwin to concentrate on writing for long periods. Although he resisted the idea that he was a spokesman, for several years Baldwin devoted most of his time and energy on civil rights, which took a toll on his artistic life.

Furthermore, as Baldwin's celebrity status rose, his lifestyle became more elaborate. Crowds of admirers always surrounded him, and there was a growing staff of secretaries, drivers, money-managers:

> Baldwin was forever gregarious and, as his celebrity-rating rose, so did the scale of his conviviality. If he had an appointment at four, he might turn up three hours late and coax the people who had patiently waited for him to accompany him to the house where he was expected at six. Then the combined parities, who had not previously known each other but by now were old friends, would be enjoined to escort him to a restaurant to keep his dinner date at nine (which he would announce, at the earliest, at ten). (Campbell 189)

Friends and strangers were attracted to his "incredibly expressive eyes and a wide mouth that flashed frequent gap-toothed smiles ... [h]is slight, erect body ... was like a frail wire connected to a big bulb that continually lit up: you noticed only the intense look of his dark face and especially the eyes" (Weatherby 153).

In 1964, *Blues for Mister Charlie* was produced by the Actor's Studio, a production rife with controversy from the beginning. Originally, Baldwin was supposed to work with Elia Kazan, who gave Baldwin the initial idea for the play, at the Actors Studio, but Kazan had moved onto Lincoln Center. When Baldwin stayed with Actors Studio instead of following Kazan, Kazan felt betrayed, but still tried to maintain their friendship. During the production of *Blues*, Baldwin developed a reputation for being melodramatic and difficult to work with. The tension between Baldwin and the theater company grew, escalating with the removal of the director Frank Corsaro. Stories of Baldwin's temper circulated wildly around Broadway. For example, one day, Baldwin climbed a 30-foot high ladder and berated the company's leader and artist director, Lee Strasberg, in front of his own company for sabotaging his play.

When *Blues* opened, the reviews were mixed, with most critics accusing the writing of being too polemical, and citing simplistic characterizations of the southern whites. When the producer announced the play's closing after its 44th performance, Baldwin was furious and reached out for support by celebrities, including Sammy Davis Jr. and Paul Newman. After the play was temporarily rescued, Baldwin took off for Europe, but by the end of the summer, due to lack of money, *Blues* closed.

To his friends, Baldwin seemed restless, uncertain what to do next. Between the summers of 1964–1965, he traveled to Paris, London, Helsinki, Rome, and Istanbul. He also bought an apartment on West 71st Street in New York, for both him and his family. He was exhausted from the past two years—from his involvement with the Civil Rights Movement, the messy production of *Blues*, and personal problems. He felt more torn about his relationship with Lucien, who was dating Diana Sands, the leading actress of *Blues*, and would later marry her. Also, Baldwin received news that his friend Beauford Delaney had had a nervous collapse in Paris and was growing delusional.

Then, on February 21, 1965, he was hit with devastating news. Baldwin was dining with his sister Gloria in London when the headwaiter called Gloria to take a phone message—reporters were on their way over: Malcolm X had been assassinated.

Malcolm had been addressing a meeting at the Audubon Ballroom on 166th Street in Harlem when he was shot. Malcolm X was no longer with the Nation of Islam. After making a pilgrimage to Mecca, the holy city of Islam, Malcolm renounced his belief that all whites were evil, and now embraced non-violence. Later, it was revealed that three Black Muslims had killed him, but the London papers reported Baldwin as shouting to reporters, "You did. You killed him. All of you!" (Campbell 207), characterizing him as being out of touch and extremist. However, when Baldwin told the reporters, "Whatever hand pulled the trigger did not buy the bullet. That bullet was forged in the crucible of the West, that death was dictated by the most successful conspiracy in the history of the world, and its name is white supremacy," he meant that the identity of the killer was not as important as the history of hatred which had created this violent climate.

After Malcolm's assassination, Baldwin joined Martin Luther King, Jr. and 25,000 others on March 25 for the great march in support of voter registration from Selma to Montgomery, Alabama; however, Malcolm's death left Baldwin feeling pessimistic and less forgiving. Although he did not always agree with Malcolm's philosophy, he admired him a great deal—his intelligence, composure, and love for blacks. With Malcolm X's assassination came an unraveling in the Civil Rights Movement. Times were changing, and America was turning its attention to the growing Vietnam War. America would never be as immersed with the racial scene as it was in the early sixties. And although Baldwin had no way of realizing it yet, he had already reached the peak of his influences, as both an artist and spokesman.

Baldwin again sequestered himself in Turkey, where he could find isolation and peace, and concentrate fully on his writing. "The principal reason that I now find myself in Istanbul is that I am a writer, and I find it easier to work here than I do elsewhere. I am left alone here," he explained (*Conversations* 59). The trip was for his writing, but it was also important that Baldwin get away from America. Although he did not know Malcolm X well, Baldwin had always admired him for his brilliance and courage, and his death left Baldwin feeling hopeless and afraid for the future of America.

Between the end of 1964 and mid-1967, Baldwin was a semi-resident in Turkey. Although Baldwin removed himself from the struggle in America, he never felt that he'd abandoned his country:

> I love America more than any other country in the world, and, exactly for this reason, I insist on the right to criticize her perpetually. I think all theories are suspect, that the finest principles may have to be modified, or may even be pulverized by the demands of life, and that one must find, therefore, one's own moral center and move through the world hoping that this center will guide one alright. I consider that I have many responsibilities, but none greater than this: to last, as Hemingway says, and get my work done. I want to be an honest man and a good writer. (*Notes of a Native Son* 9)

Baldwin was often torn between politics and writing, but the truth was, although he was a significant influence in speaking about civil rights, he was no politician—he was an artist. "I have never stopped fighting for civil rights, but I must do my work or I'll be of no use to anyone" (*Conversations* 63).

During the mid-sixties the Civil Rights Movement was taking major turns, and Baldwin was anxious to find a place in it. Violence was building, and soon Stokely Carmichael's Black Panthers filled a space left by Malcolm X. The Black Panther Party for Self Defense consisted of such young leaders as Huey P. Newton, Bobby Seale, and Eldridge Cleaver. The Panthers ran medical clinics and provided free food to school children, and also followed the motto, "By any means necessary," advocating uniforms and weapons. Baldwin first met Panther leadership in San Francisco in October, 1967, shortly after Newton was arrested for the murder of a cop. Baldwin on one hand supported the Panthers' activism, but he never embraced the idea of guns or fully swallowed the idea of separatism: "Whether I were for or against violence is absolutely irrelevant. The question that really obsesses me today is not whether or not I like violence, or whether or not you like it—unless the situation is ameliorated, and very, very quickly, there *will* be violence" (*Conversations* 12).

Whites felt Baldwin was becoming militant and radical—when Baldwin wrote an open letter "In Defense of Stokely Carmichael," the *Times* in London and the *New York Times* refused to publish it. On the other hand, many younger African-Americans felt that Baldwin's importance had shrunk and that he was now an outdated figure. They considered him too moderate and increasingly irrelevant. Young African-American intellectuals, including Ishmael Reed and Amiri Baraka, criticized Baldwin, and he was also blasted when he defended William Styron's novel *The Confessions of Nat Turner*, in which Styron, who was white, wrote from the perspective of Nat Turner, the leader of a slave revolt and black folk-hero. Baldwin, however, stuck by his support for Styron: "I will not tell another writer what to write ... He writes out of reasons similar to mine: about something which hurt him and frightened him" (*Conversations* 247).

Baldwin published very little during the mid-sixties. He did, however, involve himself in theater and film. In 1965, *The Amen Corner* had at last received a Broadway production; however, it did not make much of a sensation and played only a short run. Then Baldwin went to Los Angeles after Columbia Pictures hired him to write a screenplay on the life of Malcolm X; however, Baldwin's treatment was a manuscript of more than 200 pages that read more like a novel than a screenplay. Conflict quickly rose between Baldwin and the producers; unlike the Actors Studio, however, Columbia had no interest in trying to compromise with Baldwin. Later Baldwin said of Columbia, "It was hopeless crap. Hollywood's fantasy is designed to prove to you that this poor, doomed nitwit deserves his fate" (*Conversations* 167).

Then, on April 4, 1968, his already fragile world fell apart. Baldwin was sitting on the edge of swimming pool in Palm Springs with Billy Dee Williams, listening to Aretha Franklin on the radio and having a drink, when he got a phone call telling him that Martin Luther King had been shot. Baldwin, inconsolable, wept.

Baldwin went to the funeral in Atlanta, along with such celebrities as Sammy Davis, James Brown, Marlon Brando, Harry Belafonte, and Sidney Poitier. There seemed to be no end to the violence sweeping America. Riots spread throughout the country after King's murder, frustration and despair was overtaking many Americans' hope for the future. Then, almost a month later, Robert Kennedy was shot.

Baldwin needed to remove himself from this environment. He was devastated by King's death, and he did the only thing he could manage: he fled. For a while, he stopped writing, deeply anguished and grieving. Friends noticed the change in Baldwin—the increase in his drinking (friends recall that Baldwin usually had a glass of Johnny Walker in hand), the palpable grief and hopelessness. "For a very long time, until Martin died, I was operating as public speaker in the context of the civil rights movement," he admitted. "And when Martin died, something happened to me and something happened to many people. It took a while for me and for many people to pull ourselves back together" (*Conversations* 178).

LEAVING AMERICA

With the endless assassinations of his friends and America's leaders, Baldwin, who often self-dramatized, began to fear he would be next. "I'm the last witness—everybody else is dead. I couldn't stay in America, I had to leave," he told Ida Lewis in 1970 (*Conversations* 85). Baldwin was devastated by King's assassination. He respected King immensely, and felt that with his death, something irretrievable had been lost for America.

In Istanbul, he produced a play, *Fortune and Men's Eyes*. The play ran for several months and received rave reviews, which was a relief for Baldwin, especially after the reviews for his latest novel, *Tell Me How*

Long the Train's Been Gone, which was published in 1968, and had been disastrous. It was surprising that the play, with its homosexual content, found such success in Turkey. Baldwin was open about his homosexuality, but didn't understand why it was such an issue. "American males are the only people I've ever encountered in the world who are willing to go on the needle before they'll go to bed with each other," he stated (*Conversations* 79).

Baldwin found himself adrift since the change of the Civil Rights mood in America. He was no longer regarded as an important voice for the movement. Furthermore, his writing no longer appeared in the magazines he had once written for, including *Harper's*, *Esquire*, and *Mademoiselle*. Although he was hurt by the criticism, he refused to fully back separatism or white liberalism. "After all, I've been treated as badly by black people as I have by white people. And I'm not about to accept another kind of cultural dictatorship. I won't accept it from Governor Wallace, and I won't accept it from anybody else, either. I am an artist. No one will tell me what to do" (*Conversations* 92). In some ways, the words he once wrote about Richard Wright had come back to haunt him: in "Alas, Poor Richard" Baldwin had pointed out how young American blacks had turned away from Wright: "It must have been extremely hard to bear, and it was certainly very frightening to watch. I could not help feeling: *Be careful. Time is passing for you, too, and this may be happening to you one day*" (213).

Although it seemed to many people that Baldwin had cut himself off from politics, he was still at work. For example, he rushed to the defense of activists Stokely Carmichael and Angela Davis when they were arrested, and for seven years, Baldwin worked on a expensive campaign to have a young friend, Tony Maynard, who was falsely accused of killing a Marine in the Village, released from prison, in which he donated substantial amounts to time, money, and emotional resources.

In Paris, his whirlwind lifestyle caught up with him. After Baldwin collapsed, he was hospitalized for ten days and diagnosed with hepatitis. He was advised to give up cigarettes and alcohol, but Baldwin stubbornly believed the illness was a result of psychological stress. After he was released from the hospital, he went to recuperate in the tiny village St. Paul-de-Vence in the south of France, about ten miles from Nice. After staying in a hotel for a time, he moved into a room in a 300-year-old stone farm house, surrounded by fields and a garden. Soon, he decided to buy the house, which would be his home until he died.

Baldwin was rarely alone. Lovers, friends, and admirers swarmed around him. He had adulators who answered the phone and sorted the mail. Close friends, including Lucien, Beauford Delaney, and Bernard Hassell, a long time friend, visited; yet, still, Baldwin was lonely for a serious love and companionship, as he'd once hoped to have with Lucien. He was also depressed about the state of America. "I'm much sadder now, which doesn't mean that I'm discouraged. When you are 20 you see the world one way and when you're older you see it another way" (*Conversations* 111).

Baldwin was criticized by many for moving to the south of France and isolating himself, and his writing no longer saw the critical or popular success it once had. While his peers hit the bestseller list, such as Mailer, Styron, Roth, and Capote, Baldwin was silent. He published another book of nonfiction, *No Name in the Street*, reflecting his involvement in the Civil Rights Movement, but critics felt the spark had gone out of his writing and that after King's death, Baldwin's views had become more radical, his writing more polemical.

In 1973, he published, *If Beale Street Could Talk*, his first novel since *Tell Me How Long the Train's Been Gone*, which was six years prior. Reviews were mixed, with most critics expressing disappointment that Baldwin had not written something more ambitious. His publishers were also waiting for a major novel. Baldwin was working on a novel *Just Above my Head*, but he was having trouble finishing it. His publishers were growing anxious. Finally, his agent at the time, Jay Acton, convinced Baldwin to go to his house on Cape Cod during the summer of 1979. By September, Baldwin had completed most of the book. In this novel, published five years after *Beale Street*, Baldwin writes about love between men, and the novel is overflowing with music—spirituals and gospel, blues and jazz. *Just Above My Head* was his first commercial success in nearly fifteen years, spending 37 weeks on the *Washington Post* bestseller list. It was also to be his last published novel.

In the 1980s, Baldwin was occupied by three major projects, a novel called *No Papers for Mohammed*, a play, and a biography on Medgar Evers, Malcolm X, Martin Luther King. Unfortunately, of the projects, he was only able to finish the play, called *The Welcome Table*. Weatherby observed:

Every writer's career is filled with abandoned projects, and perhaps Baldwin at that period, when he was finding it hard to write, was just trying to boost his own confidence. The change in him, the disillusionment following King's death, certainly affected his viewpoint as a writer. The fierce idealism that had been so much a part of his writing had been largely lost with the decline of the civil rights movement. (315)

To make matters worse, Baldwin's health was declining, yet he refused to give up smoking or drinking. He had a succession of young lovers, but felt increasingly depressed about his age and his inability to complete a project. It seemed to many people that he was at the end of his writing career.

In the spring of 1981, he was given a magazine assignment to write about the child murders that had been taking place in Atlanta, Georgia for *Playboy*. A young black man, Wayne Williams, had been convicted of the crime, but many people, Baldwin among them, maintained doubts about his guilt. The article appeared in the December 1981 issues of *Playboy* and won the 1981 best Nonfiction Award. After the story, Baldwin returned to Atlanta several times during next three years, eventually turning the article into a book, *The Evidence of Things Not Seen*. Dial rejected the book, ending their long relationship with Baldwin, and then it was turned down by several other publishing houses. Henry Holt finally published the book, but it was hardly noticed in the publishing world, and the reviews were poor. Critics accused Baldwin of falling back on old material, and many felt that Baldwin had grown unconnected to his subject. Close friends, however, defended him. Dr. Kenneth Clark said, "He was influenced by what was happening and not happening in the United States. He was very, very concerned" (Weatherby 320). During the 1970s, France remained his base, but Baldwin returned frequently to the United States: "For better or for worse, my ties with my country are too deep, and my concern is too great" (*Conversations* 60).

Baldwin took a series of university teaching positions in the United States, including positions at the University of California and the University of Massachusetts. Although Baldwin never grew accustomed to the academic schedule and was notorious for showing up late to class or missing office hours, his students liked him and he was a popular teacher.

Although Baldwin no longer wielded the influence he once had in America, he still appeared in the public eye from time to time and rarely refused an interview. However, people no longer turned to Baldwin for his views on America. It was common to hear that Baldwin, spending most of his time in France, had lost touch with America of the 1980s.

One movement that was gaining ground in America during this time was the gay and lesbian movement. For his entire career, Baldwin had been opened about his sexuality, but he never aligned himself with the movement:

> All I can tell you is that, as regards for example gay liberation, I'm very glad that it seems to be easier for a boy to admit that he's in love with a boy, or for a girl to admit that she's in love with a girl, instead of, as happened in my generation, you had kids going on the needle because they were afraid that they might want to go to bed with someone of the same sex. That's part of the sexual paranoia of the United States and really of the western world. (*Conversations* 184)

At his house in France, Baldwin never rose before noon. The dinner table was usually set for at least twelve people, and the food and drink always flowed. In the 1980s, visitors continued to pass through, including Bobby Short, Miles Davis, Maya Angelou, Nina Simone, Bill Cosby, and Toni Morrison. Baldwin, trying futilely to conceal his ill health, continuously played the energetic host, but friends noticed that he "seemed to be graying rapidly and shrinking into old age, the lines on his face deeper, with almost a wizened look" (Weatherby 342).

Baldwin's final book, *The Price of the Ticket*, was published in 1985. Every one of Baldwin's essays, arranged in chronological order, are collected in this book. At the time, *The Price of the Ticket* was basically ignored by American critics, but now it is regarded as a valuable collection of Baldwin's impressive and brilliant writings. Although Baldwin had fallen out of fashion in America, in France, his adopted country, President Francois Mitterand, awarded Baldwin with the Commander of the Legion d'Honneur.

Baldwin's health began to rapidly deteriorate. He had trouble swallowing, and was diagnosed was cancer of the esophagus. After an operation in April, 1987, he gradually improved until the summer, but his liver was diseased and the cancer had spread there. Doctors told Baldwin's brother, David that the tumor was malignant, but David decided not to tell Baldwin—to let him enjoy the rest of his short life.

On December 1, 1987, Baldwin died in his bed, surrounded by his brother David, Lucien Happersberger, and Bernard Hassell, at his home in France.

In everything he did, Baldwin's voice was a voice of love. He once proclaimed, "It demands great spiritual resilience not to hate the hater whose foot is on your neck, and an even greater miracle of perception and charity not to teach your child to hate" (*The Fire Next Time* 99). In the end of his life, he seemed to reach a place where he could be at peace with himself, although there was still much he wanted to say. He had spent almost his whole life struggling against the feelings that his stepfather had planted in him, but still, no matter how despairing things seemed, Baldwin never let the hatred overcome his hope for a better world.

His funeral was held at New York Cathedral of St. John the Divine, not far from Harlem, where in 1974, he had received the award "Artist as Prophet." More than 5,000 peopled arrived at what was officially called a celebration. Famous writers, musicians, and many others whose lives he had touched paid tribute to man who once proclaimed, "I'm a witness. That's my responsibility. I write it all down" (*Conversations* 92).

WORKS CITED

Baldwin, James. *The Fire Next Time*. New York. Vintage International, 1993.

_____. *Nobody Knows My Name*. New York. Vintage International 1993

_____. *Notes of a Native Son*. Boston: Beacon Press, 1983.

Campbell, James. *Talking at the Gates: a Life of James Baldwin*. New York: Penguin Books, 1991.

Standley, Fred, and Louis H. Pratt, ed. *Conversations with James Baldwin*. Jackson: University Press of Mississippi, 1989.

Weatherby, W.J. *James Baldwin: An Artist on Fire*. New York: Donald I. Fine Inc, 1990.

GABRIEL WELSCH

James Baldwin:
Nothing Less than Courageous

What can one say after summarizing, sampling, analyzing and interpreting the work of James Baldwin and reactions to that work, except that here is a writer of exceptional range and power ... What emerges ... from the whole of his work, is a kind of absolute conviction and passion and honesty that is nothing less than courageous.

When his work is joined with his life, the picture of courage grows. As we see Baldwin now victorious against the odds of poverty, race, stature, looks, homosexuality, publishing realities for black authors, it is needful to remind ourselves of the struggle that victory represents. We must remind ourselves because Baldwin has shared his struggle with his readers for a purpose—*to demonstrate that our suffering is our bridge to one another.*

—Carolyn Wedin Sylvander

James Baldwin's work grew out of his early training as an evangelical minister, his difficulties with sexual ambiguity, his domineering and harsh father, and his keen and empathic eye for the common experiences of a variety of people, white and black. His novels and stories dealt with sexual and racial relations, the violence and suffering engendered by both, and the crucible of family, history, and society that perpetuated and witnessed suffering borne of those schisms. He expanded and sharpened, even gave shape (as some suggest) the ideas of his novels in essays, collected in several volumes, which many see as the greatest expression of his central message. As Sylvander notes in the italicized line above (the italics were added), the message is that our "suffering is our bridge to one another."

In Baldwin's call for understanding that the history of black men and women in America is the key to American history and what it means to be American, an empathy for suffering is required. In his argument, put forth in the widely acclaimed and influential volume, *The Fire Next Time*, an understanding of suffering is also required to find in oneself the love necessary to overcome racial division. In his fiction and plays, characters constantly face the challenge to make lives in spite of suffering.

Generally, Baldwin's earlier the novels, stories, and essays collected and published between 1948 and 1963 were received with greater favor than his later pieces, and his debut novel received and continues to receive the greatest praise of all his work.

GO TELL IT ON THE MOUNTAIN

Ten years in the making, *Go Tell It on the Mountain* launched Baldwin's career when it was published in 1953 to wide acclaim. The autobiographical novel told the story of John Grimes' finding the Lord in a service in a Harlem church, on a day when the tensions of his family nearly claimed the life of his half-brother and the stifling dominance of his father, Gabriel, would be tested in the very arena in which he found solace, strength, and vocation—the church. On the cusp of John's conversion in the church, the novel veers deep into the past of each of the principal adult characters, such that readers see each person's distinct suffering, failure, temptations, and crimes, the rough record of failure and struggle that led them to be standing in the Harlem church witnessing one man's beginnings. The rough details of the novel, its overbearing father, its emotionally and sexually conflicted protagonist, and the pervasive signs of a long family and racial history, parallel aspects of Baldwin's own life.

The novel contains Baldwin's first large-scale portrayal of Harlem, a topic he returned to throughout his career. John Grimes' trip downtown, early in the novel, has echoes of a descent into hell, a theme which reappears when black characters leave Harlem and venture downtown in *Another Country*, *If Beale Street Could Talk*, and *The Amen Corner*, to name a few. Not that Harlem comes off as a paradise; rather,

Harlem is a contradiction, containing the community of familiar individuals and a character's roots and family (as in Tish's case, in *If Beale Street Could Talk*), the enticement of the "real" and gritty (as it is for Vivaldo in *Another Country*), or the church and the absence of whites (the safety Gabriel returns to). Harlem is also recognizably a place people simply *must* escape, as John's brother, Gabriel's first son, does, and from which Sonny realizes he must run in "Sonny's Blues."

Go Tell It on the Mountain is based in the experience of the evangelical church. Religious allusion, imagery, critique, and tradition dominate the novel and, just as in *The Amen Corner* and *If Beale Street Could Talk*, scriptural reference peppers the work. *Go Tell It on the Mountain* contained elements that reappear through the work that followed, including instances of "trembling" and the "cup of trembling," drawn from Chapter 51 of the Book of Isaiah. The most famous instance of the "very cup of trembling" comes in the final line of the hugely influential and often anthologized story, "Sonny's Blues."

The verses specifically invoked read, in the King James version:

Awake, awake, stand up, O Jerusalem, which hast drunk at the hand of the LORD the
     cup of his fury; thou hast drunken the dregs of the cup of trembling, and wrung
          them out.

... Behold, I have taken out of thine hand the cup of trembling, even the dregs of
     the cup of my fury; thou shalt no more drink it again:
but I will put it into the hand of them that afflict thee; which have said to thy soul,
     Bow down, that we may go over: and thou has laid they body as the ground, and
          as the street, to them that went over. (Isaiah 51.17, 22–3.)

The promise of relief, redemption, and divine justice had obvious relevance for Balwin's characters. Theologian Roland E. Murphy notes, "Together, [Isaiah's chapters] present a moving vision of the assured hope of God's people in a world whose times are in God's hands." In its dealing with the destruction of the Temple and the promise of a restoration to Zion, the prophetic book resonated with preachers to whom Baldwin would have been exposed and would likely have emulated during his training. Isaiah is invoked several times in *Go Tell It on the Mountain*; the imagery of trembling occurs in several places in *Go Tell It on the Mountain*, and in numerous places in *Another Country*; and Baldwin's role as a witness and prophet turns frequently to rhetoric about a world so far gone that it is up to God and hope to save it. In 1989, two years after Baldwin's death, Maya Angelou even wrote, prophetically herself, about "James Baldwin in his role as the biblical prophet Isaiah admonishing his country to repent from wickedness and create within itself a spirit and a clean heart."

Many critics also have had their attention drawn to Baldwin's portrayal of working class, urban blacks dealing with evangelical religious elements in their lives. Trudier Harris argued, in 1996, that the novel represented the tail end of literature born in the experience of fundamentalism. Harris notes that changes in black culture, including the Black Arts movement, fostered literary work that departed from fundamentalist experience. Baldwin's treatment of the fundamentalist world had elements of reverence and blasphemy. The language of the novel mirrored and evoked the rhythms of what Baldwin himself recognized as the "King James Bible and the store front church" (something his prose would continue to do throughout his career) but the story questioned the suffering and conflicts inherent in the behavior of religious institutions and individuals.

As Harris writes, "The theme of suffering in the novel drew commentary from reviewers almost as consistently as Gabriel's destructive character. The consequences of sin and of racial oppression were the twin prongs causing that suffering ... Baldwin succeeded in drawing effectively the dilemma of an intelligent young man, on the verge of sexual and spiritual awakening, who cannot trust the person who should be his guide through both these processes." As well, he revealed the depth of comparable suffering borne by every other character in the novel, and how those deep, complex stories led to profound effects on the moment of John's transformation on the church floor.

That theme in *Go Tell It on the Mountain*—the impact of accumulated history on families and individuals—Baldwin had explored as well through the essays he wrote and published while writing the novel. In much of the work, Baldwin examined the effect of decades of neglect, hostility, and violence, not only as it related to what he called the "Negro experience," but also what effect it had on white people as well. As Odessa says in *The Amen Corner*, "men and women can come together and change each other and make each other suffer, and make each other glad." For Baldwin, if suffering can be borne, it can then unite.

In 1948 *Commentary* published "The Harlem Ghetto" as well as a short story. Other publications in both genres followed, such that by the time *Go Tell It on the Mountain* appeared, Baldwin had earned a reputation as both a fiction writer and an essayist. But his next visible work would be drama.

THE AMEN CORNER

Though not published until the sixties, *The Amen Corner* was completed and first staged, at Howard University, in 1955. The play came on the heels of the success of *Go Tell It on the Mountain*, and readers and theatre-goers saw Baldwin dealing with a similar subject and setting. It also introduced themes that would long remain familiar to Baldwin readers. In the play's three acts covering a week in time, Margaret, the pastor of a small church in Harlem, confronts the demons of her past with the return of her estranged jazz musician husband, Luke, and the coming-of-age rebellion and rejection of the church by her teenage son, David. As these personal events unfold, the elders of her church judge her as capitulating to a past life of sin and work to wrest the small church from her oversight.

Luke returns to Margaret and David's tenement home, his body wracked with illness and fatigue. He arrives just as David has started to question his own origins, his past, the church, and its relation. Among other revelations, David realizes the story his mother gave him about Luke leaving is not entirely true. Margaret left David, convinced his sinning ways were beyond hope, and wanting to save herself and her son. The church elders interpret Luke's return as the wages of a sinful past, and argue that the sin evident in her wayward son and corrupt husband are incompatible with the state of grace a pastor must possess to adequately care for her flock.

Odessa is the principal defender of Margaret to the sainted elders. As they scheme, Margaret devotes most of her attention to Luke and

David, to deal with the problems with which each has come to her. Odessa's defense of her sister is also a criticism of the elders, and one which centers on Baldwin's ideas about suffering. She says, in Act III: "Maybe I don't know the Lord like you do, but I know something else. I know how men and women can come together and change each other and make each other suffer, and make each other glad."

It is that suffering which both plagues Margaret and gives her momentary strength for bearing her husband and her son and the weight of their decisions. But it does have a cost, a cost many of Baldwin's characters lament, especially when love is either withheld or denied or ended. Margaret knows how the refusal of love, whatever form it takes, does not mean it goes away. She says, "It's a awful thing to think about, the way love never dies!"

Luke echoes the sentiment of his wife and his sister-in-law when he has his first and only heart to heart talk with his son. David comes to him with a raw need for answers, for some guidance regarding the choice to leave the church, to pursue music, to pursue life away from Harlem, a choice he has all but made already. Luke says to him, "Son—don't try to get away from the things that hurt you—sometimes that's all you got. You got to learn to live with those things—and—use them. I've seen people—put themselves through terrible torture—and die—because they was afraid of getting hurt."

Baldwin's next collected volume built on that very idea, the torture and hurt endured by people lost and persecuted, and especially for those who do not recognize their own role in it.

NOTES OF A NATIVE SON

In 1955, *Notes of a Native Son* collected several of Baldwin's essays in four sections—setting out a contemporary and nuanced view of literature, American culture, European culture, and the realities of the ghetto as they related to the "Negro problem." But he was also quick to explain his view of the "problem" in the introduction to the collection:

> I don't think that the Negro problem in America can even be discussed coherently without bearing in mind its context; its context being the history, traditions, customs, the moral assumptions and preoccupations of this country; in short, the general social fabric. Appearances to the contrary, no one in

America escapes its effects and everyone in America bears some responsibility for it. I believe this more firmly because it is the overwhelming tendency to speak of this problem as though it were a thing apart.... I love America more than any other country in the world, and, exactly for this reason, I insist on the right to criticize her perpetually.

The ideas about the "general social fabric" presaged the focus he would have in his next two novels; after writing so eloquently in *Notes of a Native Son* about the experience of being black in America, his very next novel did not have a black character in it. Baldwin defended the action against his critics as noting the novel was about another aspect of experience, that it was a love story in which the character's whiteness was important to understanding the world of privilege David risked sacrificing in his relationship with Giovanni. Given the contents and the incendiary ideas contained in *Notes of a Native Son*, critics' response to *Giovanni's Room* was not surprising. The essays ranged from his famous attacks on Richard Wright's *Native Son* ("Many Thousands Gone") and Harriet Beecher Stowe's *Uncle Tom's Cabin*, to his reportorial and prophetic essays on the realities and foundations of Harlem, to essays on the meaning and experience of being a black American, in the South and abroad.

In the essays on literature, Baldwin disdained what he called protest literature, work whose main purpose was to support an ideology and which did so through sentimental or otherwise unsophisticated technique, a charge he leveled at both Wright's and Stowe's novels. He argues that Wright's novel, by staying within the narrow parameters of Bigger Thomas's worldview, negates important elements within Negro life:

> What this means for the novel is that a necessary dimension has been cut away; this dimension being the relationship that Negroes bear to one another, that depth of involvement and unspoken recognition of shared experience which creates a way of life. What the novel reflects—and at no point interprets—is the isolation of the Negro within his own group and the resulting fury of impatient scorn. It is this which creates its climate of anarchy and unmotivated and

un-apprehended disaster; and it is this climate, common to most Negro protest novels, which has led us to believe that in Negro life there exists no tradition, no field of manners, no possibility of ritual or intercourse, such as may, for example, sustain the Jew even after he has left his father's house. But the fact is not that the Negro has no tradition but that there has as yet arrived no sensibility sufficiently profound and tough to make this tradition articulate.

As he critiqued the novels, he also set forth his own criteria for good literature, stating that humanity was too complicated to conform to the restrictions of thematically driven stories. For Baldwin, fidelity to character and the verity of the story were paramount, and not to be sacrificed due to a contrivance so that the author could make a point.

His call for truth extended to his reportorial essays on Harlem. Baldwin wrote frequently that he saw his role as one of "witness." In *No Name in the Street*, written when his role as a witness was arguably more public and of greater exigency, he wrote, "That's my responsibility. I write it all down." In the early essays, leading up to the hugely influential *The Fire Next Time*, Baldwin's work as witness revealed to generally stunned white readers the reality of being black in the United States. While black readers and critics found they recognized much of what Baldwin wrote, there were those who felt Baldwin overstepped his role when he criticized black leaders and politicians or blacks themselves. Baldwin's position throughout such complaints about his work was that for the truth to have any relevance or impact it could not be selective.

As he notes about the protest novel, this time in an essay about *Uncle Tom's Cabin*, "The failure of the protest novel lies in its rejection of life, the human being, the denial of his beauty, dread, power, in its insistence that it is his categorization alone which is real and which cannot be transcended." Thus, the collection's essays on Harlem, the South, life abroad in France, and so on, essays considering the experience of being Negro and American in a variety of places, work very hard to present an accurate and balanced report. In "The Harlem Ghetto," Baldwin both criticizes and sympathizes with community leaders whose well-meaning gestures simply fling them back into other battles, often ones over the very "improvements" (like housing projects) a version of which they had earlier fought to gain. In "Encounter on the Seine," Baldwin reflects on how it took leaving his country to realize his particular American identity. On meeting African men and women in France, he realized that the power of his home asserted over him an identity that meant he had more history and identity in common with white bigots than with people whose skin had the same hue as his own.

Thus, one important crux of the early collection is Baldwin's thinking about the "Negro problem in America." If anything, the collection argues for nuance, for the consideration of culture, for the importance of bearing honest witness:

> The story of the Negro in America is the story of America—or, more precisely, it is the story of Americans. It is not a very pretty story: the story of a people is never very pretty. The Negro in America, gloomily referred to as that shadow which lies athwart our national life, is far more than that. He is a series of shadows, self-created, intertwining, which now we helplessly battle. One may say that the Negro in America does not really exist except in the darkness of our minds.

Finally, as Horace Porter points out, "Baldwin explores the significance of his father's life and death. And through that process, he discovers something about the nature of the hatred and bitterness he carries in his own heart." His admission of culpability, of carrying hate himself, as well as his acknowledgment that one cannot ignore the past and the burden of family and heritage, transform his criticisms and reportage into something finer, prophetic, forward looking, as if the admission was purgative, and would be for readers writ large, were they to possess the strength and ability for such introspection. Fittingly, Baldwin's next book would feature a narrator nearly paralyzed with the burden of introspection and worrying at what kind of world his actions and self-loathing will cost him.

GIOVANNI'S ROOM

Giovanni's Room was published in 1956 and remains Baldwin's most controversial work. The homosexual relationships frankly presented in the book attracted pointed criticism, and many black writers noted that the book contained only white characters. Baldwin's response was defiant; for him, whiteness was a critical aspect of the story. He also felt that the core of the story demanded that no concession be made on the two components that attracted the criticism.

In the novel, David lives in Paris and is in the midst of a difficult pause in his relationship with Hella, a woman to whom he is engaged. Due to unresolved tensions between them, Hella leaves David to spend time in Spain for a while. During her absence, David begins an affair with a young Italian man, Giovanni. The two live in a small room in a larger house for which Giovanni is a caretaker. Decorated with an oversized and sentimental painting of a man and woman in the throes of romance, the room is otherwise a shambles, described variously as a prison, a retreat, a constrained space, and a ruin. For David, the affection and lust he feels for Giovanni is a torment because he is restrained by conventional views of manliness, sex, and love. At the same time, Giovanni's passion is overbearing, intense, jealous, and nearly violent. When Hella returns and David feels compelled to "return" to his life, to what he regards as the foregone conclusion of marriage and a typical life, Giovanni's despondence leads to suicide. Hella learns about the affair and is appalled at David's betrayal as well as what she sees as his perversion. In the end, David feels destroyed by the burden of what was expected of him, of the betrayals he committed, and of the two ruined lives left in his wake.

In *Giovanni's Room*, Baldwin covers some of his familiar thematic ground: the novel meditates on American identity, as its expatriate protagonist mulls over the very nature of his masculinity, a cipher for American identity as he understands it. Also, the impact of collective and individual history makes David's decisions fraught and destructive. He is ultimately able to feel regret through the suffering he himself endures and survives. However, some critics cite *Giovanni's Room* as the premiere example of what Hélène Christol termed, in 1991, Baldwin's "pervasive misogyny." "For Baldwin," she writes, "[women] are essentially useful mediums or symbols which he develops in a traditional way, reproducing the sexual and mythical roles of his times." She goes on to consider how Hella is threatening, soft, and how imagery of her "consuming" or "eating" David represented a deep fear of women and an attitude that found them predatory and destructive:

> Baldwin's conception of male/female relations places women at their traditional place, at the bottom of the power structure, the victims not only of cultural, social or racial

conditions, but also of some kind of biological destiny. In most of his theoretical developments of women, Baldwin seems to make no difference between sex and gender, a distinction he is perfectly able to make when dealing with manhood and masculinity.

In short, Christol points out, Baldwin's overriding themes of disparity and power with regard to masculinity and race fall apart when applied to women in his work.

Taken together, *Go Tell It on the Mountain* and *Giovanni's Room* each explore the effect of an individual "discovering identity," both racial and national, as James Oliver Horton wrote in 1991. Horton's thesis moved beyond the search in the novels and compared it to Baldwin's own search for an identity as a black intellectual and artist. Horton notes that while Baldwin followed in the steps of and owed some intellectual debts to Richard Wright, Ralph Johnson, Alain Lock and other figures of the Harlem Renaissance with regard to the discrepancy between American ideals and black realities, Baldwin's concern about the discovery of personal identity being a necessary first step toward true black liberation was a perspective uniquely his. But Baldwin understood that an *individual's* quest was perhaps the more explosive, contentious, and surprisingly contradictory endeavor. As well, Horton notes that Baldwin's powerful and central argument follows that "America's national identity is intimately bound to Afro-Americans. The nation is what it is because black people have historically been a part of the national experience.... notions of America as a 'white man's country' were never more than mythology."

NOBODY KNOWS MY NAME: MORE NOTES OF A NATIVE SON

In 1961, *Nobody Knows My Name: More Notes of a Native Son* appeared, collecting essays Baldwin wrote while in the American South on commission from *Harper's* magazine, as well as pieces that had appeared in *Partisan Review*, *Encounter*, *Harper's Mademoiselle*, and other magazines. Many critics and writers—among them Norman Mailer and Harold Bloom—have claimed his achievements in the essay revolutionized the form, a decade or more before the advent of the so-called New Journalism. Many were making the claim just before and shortly after the appearance of *Nobody Knows My Name*. Critics noted Baldwin's ability to move from his own personal and even idiosyncratic experiences to talk calmly, convincingly, and prophetically about Black experience writ large. Sylvander noted how "Baldwin's essays effectively use traditional rhetorical devices of metaphor, parallelism, repetition, and develop a characteristic autobiographical, organic growth from experience to idea." His ability to progress from one very different rhetorical mode to another set the stage for the changes in the genre that led to the literary essay as we conceive of it today. In fact, Mel Watkins made the claim specifically in 1989: "[Baldwin's] essay style, in fact, set a literary precedent, and when a similar approach was employed by Norman Mailer, Tom Wolfe, and others, it was hailed as 'New Journalism.'"

In 1977, a good decade into the revolutionary prose trend of New Journalism (the movement where journalists began using the techniques of fiction writers to write more evocative stories about factual matters) but twenty years before the sweeping phenomenon of creative nonfiction and memoir, Nick Aaron Ford wrote on what distinguished Baldwin as an essayist. Ford wrote, "The most unique feature of his style is his tendency to tie in his personal life and experiences with whatever commentary he offers on social and philosophical questions. In other words, his caustic criticisms of local, national, and world conditions result directly or indirectly from his personal experiences. He, therefore, speaks with an authority that most essayists reject as not sufficiently objective." Alfred Kazin, as well, noted, "the 'I,' the 'James Baldwin' who is sassy and despairing and bright, manages, without losing his authority as the central speaker, to show us all the different people hidden in him, all the voices for whom the 'I' alone can speak."

Watkins's, Ford's, and Kazin's writing clearly predate the modern acceptance and even valorization of personal experience as a requisite for modern essays. Given how many writers and activists have followed Baldwin's example and written memoirs and essays critical of different societies (think of Mark Methabane and *Kaffir Boy*; Richard Rodriguez's *Aria: Memoirs of a Bilingual Childhood*; Maya Angelou's *I Know Why The Caged Bird Sings*, and many, many others), it is hard to appreciate the rarity of Baldwin's rhetorical technique for the time. But the technique, as discussed earlier, was important because of how it allowed Baldwin to remain credible and authoritative to his black audience while inviting white audiences to view the world through his eyes and trust that what they saw was the truth.

In 1986, Harold Bloom outlined a claim for Baldwin as "the most considerable moral essayist now writing in the United States," noting his "evangelical heritage," his preacher's "fervor," and, finally, what separates Baldwin from Emerson—the former lacks the latter's "luxury of detachment." Baldwin is *one of* and a *voice for* "a sexual minority within a racial minority, indeed for an aesthetic minority among black homosexuals." Baldwin himself noted, in "Autobiographical Notes," at the beginning of *Notes of a Native Son*, "The difficulty ... of being a Negro writer was the fact that I was, in effect, prohibited from examining my own experience too closely by the tremendous demands and the very real dangers of my social situation."

Despite the dangers, Baldwin's reportage was unflinching. He was equally savage in his portrayal of black hypocrisy as he was with white, but perhaps was most memorably so in *The Fire Next Time*, wherein he reported an encounter with the charismatic leader of the Nation of Islam, Elijah Muhammad. *The Fire Next Time* resulted in his being on the cover of *Time* magazine as a spokesperson for civil rights, and in the conception of most of his critics, drew a clear line bisecting his career.

THE FIRE NEXT TIME

In 1963, writing about *The Fire Next Time*, Howard Levant noted that "artistic power, not the facts alone, shocks the Caucasian 'out of his skin' by forcing him to enter the artistic construct, the feeling of being a Negro in America, both in the reading and remembering the reading." Levant identified the way Baldwin's essays work. He earns the readers trust initially with personal appeal and anecdotes, such that once the reader identifies with the wise and eloquent teller of the story, whose identity initially is rendered effectively neutral by print and the distance from a bodily presence, the reader experiences the emotional impact of the facts and their arrangement through the perspective of the writer.

The Fire Next Time opens with a brief letter to Baldwin's nephew, on the centennial of the emancipation proclamation. The core of the essay is that real emancipation has yet to be realized in America. His tone is calm, his claims devastating, that the boy has been born into and placed into a "ghetto in which, in fact, [America] intended that you should perish." Baldwin's measured eloquence is, however, unsparing. The news in the short letter is grim. The longer essay which dominates the rest of the book builds from the calm tone provided at the outset.

In "Down at the Cross," Baldwin proceeds from his meditation on the limitations imposed on him by his early religious training to a consideration of the Nation of Islam and, in particular, its leader, Elijah Muhammad. As he considers Christianity, he notes its hypocrisy throughout history and the fact, from his perspective, that "the passion with which we loved the Lord was a measure of how deeply we feared and distrusted and, in the end, hated almost all strangers, always, and avoided and despised ourselves."

His appraisal of the Nation of Islam cited many similarities. His portrayal of Muhammad acknowledged the man's charisma, intellectual prowess, ease of reasoning and more. But he also noted that at the heart of Muhammad's argument and indeed at the credo of the Nation of Islam lay denial and a fallacy. Baldwin wrote:

> In order to change the situation one has first to see it for what it is: in the present case, to accept the fact, whatever one does with it thereafter, that the Negro has been formed by this nation, for better or for worse, and does not belong to any other—not to Africa, and certainly not to Islam. The paradox—and a fearful paradox it is—is that the American Negro can have no future anywhere, on any continent, as long as he is unwilling to accept his past.

He ultimately warned that the consequences of separatism, militancy, hate, and the effort to enforce de facto segregation, by both sides, would only come to erupt in violence. He warned not only white America, but black America as well, that love, understanding, and honesty were the only means possible to achieve any change.

For his effort, the FBI opened a file on him, which swelled at one point to 1750 pages. In the next few years, Baldwin would provide J. Edgar Hoover much more to get excited about.

GOING TO MEET THE MAN

Going to Meet the Man appeared in 1965, with its incendiary title story fueling the still nascent fire of militancy accusations leveled at

Baldwin. The story takes place on a night when a Southern sheriff, Jessie, is unable to sleep or perform sexually with his wife. As he lies awake, he remembers the physical excitement he experienced earlier in the day while beating a black voting rights demonstrator. As he considers the man in the cell from the day, he also remembers how, as a young boy of eight, he witnessed a horrific castration and immolation of a black man for the crime of knocking down an older white woman. His father and mother brought him to what he had thought would be a picnic. His recalled descriptions of his father make clear the man took the same sexual gratification in the death and sexual disfigurement of blacks as the sheriff now does. The story's most controversial point—that hatred and violence provided whites a sexual gratification they themselves had suppressed and channeled into only the most desperate form of release—would be approached in some of Baldwin's later essays on American sexuality, masculinity, and personal repression.

The collection also included two other much discussed stories. "The Rockpile" deals with the Grimes family, from *Go Tell It on the Mountain*, as though it were simply an excised bit turned into story form. The role of the mother is somewhat changed, as in the story she works to protect her children from Gabriel, inspiring the kids to conspire against the father so they might protect her from what their inchoate sense tells them is a far worse punishment she endures from him when she intervenes.

But the most anthologized, discussed, and famous of the stories in *Going to Meet the Man* is "Sonny's Blues." John M. Reilly wrote, in 1970, "The fundamental movement of 'Sonny's Blues' represents the slow accommodation of a first-person narrator's consciousness to the meaning of his younger brother's way of life. The process leads Baldwin's readers to a sympathetic engagement with the young man by providing a knowledge of the human motives of the youths, whose lives normally are reported to others only by their inclusion of statistics of school dropout rates, drug usage, and unemployment."

In "Sonny's Blues," the narrator—an older, stable brother, a school teacher and advocate for responsibility, for "thinking about the future"—tries to understand his younger brother's quest to be a musician, troubles with addiction, and rage. Only after the narrator sees his brother play, sees his expression mature before him, sees that his brother has drunk "from the very cup of trembling" and plays in the awful promise implied in the cast shadow, does he realize his brother is banking on spiritual redemption, on something he has to reach that is beyond this world. It is not a call for the church or for religion; rather, the story's complex ending signals Baldwin's troubled faith, something that supersedes the problems of religion as Baldwin saw it expressed and functioning on earth.

More than anything else, "Sonny's Blues" addressed suffering and Baldwin's idea of it being the bridge that connects people. When the narrator sees his brother after the death of Grace, his daughter, "I had begun, finally, to wonder about Sonny, about the life that lived inside. This life, whatever it was, had made him older and thinner and it had deepened the distant stillness in which he had always moved. He looked very unlike my baby brother. Yet, when he smiled, when we shook hands, the baby brother I'd never known looked out at me from the depths of his private life, like an animal waiting to be coaxed into the light."

Later, Sonny watches a woman singing in the street in front of the church across from his mother's apartment. Telling his brother about it, he says, "listening to that woman sing, it struck me all of a sudden how much suffering she must have had to go through—to sing like that. It's *repulsive* to think you have to suffer that much."

But when the narrator sees his brother play, he knows the young man has suffered, has borne it, however he had tried to squelch the feeling with heroin and booze. The narrator feels that people have to take it, endure it knowing it will pass, and make the best of it. Sonny, however, believes in the necessity of fighting it, and that all people *want* to fight it, want *not* to suffer. Neither viewpoint triumphs in the story, revealing Baldwin's discomfort with moral certainty and belief in the importance of truly portraying moral difficulty in his work. But it also shows suffering as the thing which brings the two together, to an edgy understanding, at the end of the story.

BLUES FOR MISTER CHARLIE

Blues for Mister Charlie was written and produced nine years after the widely publicized (in the black press and communities) murder and mutilation of Emmett Till. As such, many balked at the notion of a "blues" for a white man as written by a black author ("Mister Charlie," as the play makes clear, was a derogatory term blacks used in reference to whites.).

A fifteen-year-old boy, Till was thought to have flirted inappropriately with a white girl in a roadside store in Mississippi, to the extent that several onlookers hunted down, murdered, and mutilated him. The plot to *Blues for Mister Charlie* parallels many of the specifics of the Till case. A black man, Richard Henry, returns home to the south after drug addiction ruins a potentially solid career as an entertainer. His return seeks a kind of rebirth, which becomes possible in a romantic relationship. He then runs into Lyle Britten, a merchant and a brute whose past includes raping a black woman and killing her husband, both of which are not prosecuted by local white law enforcement. The two tangle, and Britten kills Richard for "sins" similar to those of Emmett Till; Henry's taunting suggested "economic and sexual superiority," as Carlton Molette wrote in 1977.

When Richard's murder comes out and Lyle is tried, his wife claims Richard tried to assault her. A second eyewitness lies to corroborate the wife's story, which he knows to be false. While Parnell, the town newspaper editor, considers himself generally on the side of blacks, it is only his and the white community's perception; the black characters, and the viewers of the play, see his transparency. The play's ultimate message, thus, is that blacks cannot wait for the rest of the world to either understand them or to help them change their situation. In effect, blacks must protect themselves and force change how they can. For many whites, then, despite the climate of protest marches, so-called militancy, extreme and expressive artworks, and excoriating rhetoric, the play was seen as one of the more militant works of the day, arguably because of Baldwin's high national profile and his previous popularity achieved with *The Fire Next Time*. It also didn't help matters for Baldwin's reputation that the play was published and produced right after the appearance of *Going to Meet the Man* and its horrific and controversial title story.

TELL ME HOW LONG THE TRAIN'S BEEN GONE

Tell Me How Long The Train's Been Gone has drawn the least critical attention of all Baldwin's novels. It shares many elements with stronger works—*Go Tell It on the Mountain, Another Country,* and *If Beale Street Could Talk*, but many have cited it as melodramatic, thin, and suffering from conclusions not supported by its narrative. Perhaps it has something to do with what Mario Puzo said about it in the *New York Times* in June, 1968, labeling it "a simpleminded, one-dimensional novel with mostly cardboard characters."

The novel deals with the life of Leo Proudhammer, another artist protagonist, following six years after Vivaldo and Rufus of *Another Country*, and after Richard Henry in *Blues for Mister Charlie*. The novel introduces readers to the life of Leo, his years in Harlem, and Baldwin's typically strong portrayal of family life, the grit of the ghetto, the churches, and another domineering religious father. The time in Harlem comes out of flashbacks within a narrative about Leo's fame on the stage.

When he flees Harlem, he ends up in a Greenwich Village apartment with a white, unmarried couple, Barbara and Jerry. Leo has discovered his bisexuality and amid the three individuals' struggle for success as actors, Leo and Barbara find one another and begin an affair. Puzo points out that Jerry, pretty much incredibly, is hurt but understanding.

While the affair is doomed, Leo and Barbara remain friends. Leo moves on to find a measure of happiness with a young black militant named Christopher, a figure with similarities to Malcolm X, whom Baldwin knew well. Leo buys into Christopher's militancy and calls for violence. He suffers a heart attack at the end of the novel, from which Barbara helps him to heal while declaring her love for him. Puzo writes, "We are asked to believe that the only man in the world she can love forever is a Negro homosexual actor. This is a romantic condescension equal to anything in *Gone With the Wind*, in that Baldwin does not recognize a parallel revolution, the feminine against the masculine world. In the conception of Barbara's character, in the undying devotion speech, Baldwin glorifies a sexual Uncle Tom." As Puzo's remarks imply, the novel has elements that would well support many of Christol's claims regarding misogyny. Fortunately, Baldwin would follow the novel in three years with the scintillating books of essays, *No Name in the Street*, and his work on the film version of the *Autobiography of Malcolm X*, a film project scuttled and avoided until several years after his death.

No Name in the Street

Adding to the already distinguished contribution Baldwin had made to the Civil Rights Movement, the evolution of the essay in American letters, and the role of the moral essayist in a time of relativism, *No Name in the Street*, coming on the heels of the poorly received *Tell Me How Long the Train's Been Gone*, cemented for many critics the feeling that Baldwin would leave his most profound mark as an essayist.

The book chronicled a number of Baldwin's experiences during the Civil Rights Movement and included lengthy meditations on prominent figures including Martin Luther King, Jr., Malcom X, and Medgar Evers. As well, it continued the philosophical discussions started in his three earlier volumes of essays, on the basis for white attitudes toward blacks, on the worrisome aspects of militancy and separation, and on the need for love to overcome the challenges of the age:

> Nakedness has no color: this can come as news only to those who have never covered, or been covered by, another naked human being.... In any case, the world changes then, and it changes forever. Because you love one human being, you see everyone else very differently than you saw them before—perhaps I only mean to say that you begin to *see*—and you are both stronger and more vulnerable, both free and bound. Free, paradoxically, because, now, you have a home—your lover's arms. And bound: to that mystery, precisely, a bondage which liberates you into something of the glory and suffering of the world.

Of course, the other part of Baldwin's thesis regarding the need for love was the inability of Americans to love another person due to deep-seated self-loathing.

> I have always been struck, in America, by an emotional poverty so bottomless, and a terror of human life, of human touch, so deep, that virtually no American appears able to achieve a viable, organic connection between his public stance and his private life. This is what makes them so baffling, so moving, so exasperating, and so untrustworthy. 'Only connect,' Henry James has said. Perhaps only an American writer would have been driven to say it, his very existence being so threatened by the failure, in most American lives, of the most elementary and crucial connections.... If Americans were not so terrified of their

private selves, they would never have needed to invent and
could never have become so dependent on what they still call
"the Negro problem."

For many of the essays, Baldwin traveled and wrote on commission for
different groups and editors. As a result, he could afford to travel
extensively throughpout the South. The essays reveal how he was struck
by the cultural bases for manhood, born in what he saw as a hostile
territory in the South. While he expressed horror at the poverty and
oppression of the south, he contrasted the "excrescences" of commercial
excess (in a very long list running from billboards to greasy roadside
foodstands) against the aching beauty of a land described in terms of
fecundity and lushness he labeled the South's "miasma of lust and
longing and rage."

Horace Porter noted that Baldwin, as a Northern writer, saw the
South differently than many other black writers. While Baldwin himself
notes, in *Notes of a Native Son*, that many Blacks of his time referred to
the South as "the Old Country," Horace Porter shows "the South serves
as the epitome of repressive physical and psychological horror for
Baldwin."

Beyond his experiences in the South, Baldwin also writes about the
murder of Martin Luther King, his work with and sorrow over the death
of Medgar Evers, and his understanding of Malcolm X. Baldwin's
portrait of the Nation of Islam figure is particularly notable. Baldwin
examines Malcolm X's rhetoric, style, and use of various appeals in his
writings and speeches, and muses to what degree his own thinking was
affected by Malcolm X. He also compares the relative sobriety of
Malcolm X to the style and ideas of Elijah Muhammad.

In sum, Baldwin argues that Malcolm X was not a racist; rather,
saw himself as a spiritual product of the people who produced him, not
a "messiah" but a servant. Given his earlier reflections on the culture
that produced the Southern white bigot as well as the self-loathing
populations of blacks, the argument for environment extended to Civil
Rights leaders was perhaps inevitable in the volume. But Baldwin argues
further that Malcolm X's understanding of his role as a servant meant he
was willing to die to serve the people that created him. Thus, the effect
of Malcolm X was due to love. Baldwin explains: "What made [Malcolm
X] unfamiliar and dangerous was not his hatred for white people but his
love for blacks, his apprehension of the horror of the black condition,

and the reasons for it, and his determination so to work on their hearts and minds that they would be enabled to see their condition and change it themselves."

IF BEALE STREET COULD TALK

Trudier Harris noted that Baldwin's 1974 novel, *If Beale Street Could Talk* "moves its focus away from characters who are inside the church, or who have grown up in it, to characters who have consistently rejected its influence on their lives." The novel concerns Tish and Fonny, a young couple each from Harlem who are about to have a child together when Fonny is jailed on false accusations he raped a white woman. An artist, Fonny is rejected by his sainted mother and sisters, and his father is indifferent until his son is jailed. Tish's family, however, tries to help. Tish's older sister, an activist, and her father, a sober dock worker, are particularly helpful in trying to work the connections they have in the secular, downtown climate of the city to help gain Fonny's release from prison.

In the novel, the church-going characters are nearly farcical. Where *Go Tell It on the Mountain* rendered the experience of the church, testifying, and conversion as miraculous and nearly magical incidents and the church itself as a lure and salvation, however flawed, in *If Beale Street Could Talk*, most portrayals of devout characters are violent, comic, absurd, and malicious.

The acrimony of the characters for white society is more pronounced than in previous novels. However, the character's distrust and disdain for whites is tempered by the efficacy and genuine altruism of Fonny's lawyer, Hayward. While admittedly young and naïve, Hayward also becomes dogged in pursuit of ways to free Fonny, culminating in sending Tish's mother, Sharon, to Puerto Rico to get his accuser to admit her statement and identification of Fonny was a lie.

> I've got to be able to visit Fonny every instant that I can. Joseph is working overtime, double time, and so is Frank. Ernestine has to spend less time with her children because she has taken a job as a part-time private secretary to a very rich and eccentric young actress, whose connections she intends to intimidate, and use. Joseph is coldly,

systematically, stealing from the docks, and Frank is stealing from the garment center and they sell the hot goods in Harlem, or in Brooklyn. They don't tell us this, but we know it. They don't tell us because, if things go wrong, we can't be accused of being accomplices. We cannot penetrate their silence, we must not try. Each of these men would gladly go to jail, blow away a pig, blow up a city, to save their progeny from the jaws of this democratic hell.

The novel brought together several of Baldwin's themes in a long work for the first time in the six years since *Tell Me How Long the Train's Been Gone*. Here, too, was a malevolent city, a place where only Greenwich Village could reasonably harbor outcasts like Tish and Fonny, Vivaldo and Ida. Here, too, was a couple whose love had to fight against obstacles, such that culture and society kept it from being completely fulfilled. As well, fathers were combinations of authority and failure, quiet love and harsh words. Harlem and, indeed, all of New York was a hell, what Tish calls early on the worst city in the world. But against their disillusionment, cynicism, and despair, they remain quintessential Baldwin characters due to what Mel Watkins calls their representation as "ordinary blacks who, though they may have considered the course taken by [Richard Wright's brutish] Bigger [Thomas], have instead resisted that temptation and affirmed their own humanity by living their lives within a complex social milieu that is virtually unknown to whites."

In 1978, Louis H. Pratt wrote:

In Baldwin's novels, love is often extended, frequently denied, seldom fulfilled. As reflections of our contemporary American society, the novels stand as forthright indictments of the intolerable conditions that we have accepted unquestioningly as a way of life. Injustices upon injustices have been perpetrated and imposed upon innocent heads until the human psyche—black and white alike—has become perverted and corrupt. In this atmosphere love cannot survive. We have substituted illusion for reality and cruelty and indifference for love, and our values have become hollow and meaningless. Moments of love, Baldwin seems to say, are precious, rare occasions to be cherished, and we must create an atmosphere where they can survive and flourish. We must find the means of reestablishing a genuine concern for the fate of our brothers. We must discover that 'other country' within the depths of ourselves so that love can again become a possibility in our lives.

Trudier Harris noted that Baldwin marks the end of African-American literature born in the experience of Christian Fundamentalism. According to Harris, after Baldwin, with a few exceptions, African American literature had its formative roots in the Civil Rights era, or in emancipation, but seldom in religion. In a way, *If Beale Street Could Talk* represents itself a shift away from the church's effect as a supportive organ for black communities to one, by the time the novel was written, that contributed to the corrosive denial of many people.

FINAL WORKS: THE DEVIL FINDS WORK; RAPPING; JUST ABOVE MY HEAD; AND EVIDENCE OF THINGS SEEN

Baldwin's sixth and longest novel, *Just Above My Head*, has, like the novel before it, yielded little study. It dealt with the fate of another artist, with Harlem, and had moving passages about the influence of music, but has been generally ignored. As well, *The Devil Finds Work*, a three-chapter essay continuing his focused thinking about American culture and civil rights in relation (this time) to film and his experiences with the industry in working on the Malcolm X project, did not generate much attention, paling as it did against the forceful volumes preceding it.

He had also published two "raps," one each with Margaret Mead and Nikki Giovanni in the early seventies, as part of a short-lived trend wherein a publisher would record an informal conversation between scholar-celebrities and publish, largely unedited, the exchange. Most critics rejected the unformed and not wholly interesting thoughts of such dialogues as worthless. Richard Elman noted, of the Margaret Mead rap (titled a "dialogue" by the publisher), "I think we better start talking to each other and stop listening to wise men and women among us except when they deign to write down what they have to say in novels and plays and poems and essays and yes, then revise, if necessary."

The Evidence of Things Not Seen came out in 1983, and was a New Journalism-style exploration of the unsolved murder of 28 black children in Atlanta in 1980 and 1981. Baldwin had taken the work as an assignment for *Playboy*, and would publish work on American masculinity in the same magazine two years later, but critics have leveled the charge that Baldwin treated the task as more essay than journalism, when the topic deserved and demanded better, more focused treatment. As John Flemming noted in the *New York Times* in November, 1985, "There is far too much sermonizing here on the overall state of race relations in America and not enough digging into specific facts of the Atlanta murders. Nonetheless, when Mr. Baldwin steps down from the pulpit he can still bring passionate intensity to reportage." While the pulpit remark was a cheap and easy swipe, the note still foretells what was going to happen to Baldwin's reputation in the few years before and after his death.

THE STATE OF BALDWIN STUDIES

In 1985, with Baldwin working on a new play (the never finished "The Welcome Table") and still teaching and lecturing, his legacy was not yet played out, and no illness was in sight. He was revered, debated, widely published, and still culturally relevant, despite the generally unfavorable reception of his works since *The Fire Next Time*. In a way, critics were still awaiting what he would finally do. For that reason, in 1985, only three book-length studies of his work had been published, along with a few dozen essays, the usual reviews, and little else. But, two years after his death in 1987, Baldwin studies exploded, first with the appreciations and collected essays that appeared through the early nineties, then a series of studies looking at various facets (like Harris' work on black women in his fiction and Porter's consideration of his "art and protest"). Finally, beginning in 2000, a number of "reassessments" began to appear, offering new insights on the most studied works (*Go Tell It on the Mountain, Notes of a Native Son, Giovanni's Room, Going to Meet the Man*) as well as critical "re-views" of the later and ignored work.

In fact, D. Quentin Miller edited a collection of essays, *Re-Viewing James Baldwin* (2000), in which he made the argument that advances in literary study made it not only possible but now necessary to look at the whole range and complexity of Baldwin, to take stock of the total artist and not simply the essayist or novelist, the Civil Rights activist or bisexual, the polemicist or dramatist.

In his introduction to the volume, Miller pinpoints the moment that American liberal acceptance began to elude Baldwin, and what the effect was on the work itself.

> ... speaking right out of the tradition of Martin Luther King, Jr., perhaps flavored by a bit of Malcolm X, he warned us that those of us—black and white—who were liberal enough could prevent the fire by working together for justice.

> But then came the terrifying short story, "Going to Meet the Man," in which a lynching is somehow associated with the sexual problems of a white sheriff, and the even more bothersome play, *Blues for Mister Charlie*, in which there seems to be an insurmountable barrier between Black Town and White Town and the black preacher at the end of the play, Malcolm X style, has a gun in his Bible. People— especially white people—were made uncomfortable by those works and they found it convenient to blame the discomfort on the author's failing powers rather than on the real problem that faced us in the mid-sixties....

> So Baldwin became disillusioned, and he expressed that disillusionment in the works that included Tish in *If Beale Street Could Talk*, Black Christopher in the autobiographical *Tell Me How Long the Train's Been Gone*, in the tragic lives of Arthur, Jimmy, and Julia, in the much underrated—in fact, ignored—family blues epic, *Just Above My Head* ... And he expresses it in the late prose works, in which critics almost uniformly have been bothered by his "unreasonable bitterness." In fact, Baldwin was never bitter; he was, as Maya Angelou has reminded us, just angry—angry about the plight of the inner-city black, angry about the sacrifice of so many modern "buffalo soldiers" in the Vietnam War and black children in the drug war, and angry about a "new South" that masked old injustices with architectural and economic glitz. He expressed his anger in several late works of nonfiction—*The Devil Finds Work, No Name in the Street*, and *The Evidence of Things Not Seen*, all segments of an

autobiography that began with the first two books of essays
and *The Fire Next Time.*

Elsewhere in the same volume, David Leeming, Baldwin's former
assistant and official biographer, made a case as well for considering all
of Baldwin, and particularly the later work. The popular stance around
the time of Baldwin's death was that the writer had become so
embittered by what he perceived as the lack of progress on race issues in
America that his later work suffered under the burden of excessive rage
and cynicism. Leeming, however, wrote that White America actually
feared the discomfort arising from the truth in Baldwin's later work.
Leeming argues that those critics resorted to arguing that Baldwin had
lost his artistic focus, thus failing to live up to the promise of his earlier
novels.

Certainly, attacks such as those by Eldridge Cleaver and LeRoi
Jones were part of one kind of reaction—each man's shrill attacks were
largely homophobic and sexist diatribes easily seen today as bluster. But
other influential critics were presenting arguments with greater nuance
about how Baldwin had abandoned his wise writing about suffering,
about identity, and about America in favor of devastating and fatalistic
critiques.

In 2002, Lynn Orilla Scott argued that there was indeed a "new
direction" in Baldwin's later novels, but it was one that built on the
earlier themes Baldwin explored. The later novels, then, can be seen
almost as a logical extension of Baldwin's thematic concerns. Scott
writes that there are "three interconnected themes that link these works
to his early essays and fiction. They are the role of the family in
sustaining the artist; the price of success in American society; and the
struggle of the black artist to change the ways sex and race are
represented in American culture." At the same time, Scott posits,
Baldwin's thematic *consistency* and wide concerns distinguished him
from other mid-century writers, and particularly from mid-century
black writers. Scott also points out how little has been noted on the
difficulties Baldwin's sexuality played in the reception of his work and
the later critical understanding of his work.

A very few critics, Trudier Harris the most visible among them,
have started to look at Baldwin's use and treatment of women in his
work. Hélène Christol notes that Baldwin's "pervasive misogyny" is a
theme throughout his work, arguing that Baldwin's themes of disparity

and power as seen in masculinity and in racial contexts actually fall apart when one considers how women fare in the novels and stories.

The most recent book-length study, Clarence E. Hardy III's 2003 *James Baldwin's God*, charts the newest territory in Baldwin studies, considering the contradictions and connections between religious fervor and sexual ecstasy in black evangelical culture as shown in different ways throughout Baldwin's work.

Most of the scholars working in the last five years have expressed a dedication to the re-birth of Baldwin studies they perceive in general. They are concerned over what new developments in cultural studies, queer theory, feminist studies, and more might consider that has been left out of the critical consideration of Baldwin to date.

Wole Soyinka summarized Baldwin's legacy in the forward to the collection Quincy Troupe edited in 1989, *James Baldwin: The Legacy*:

> James Baldwin was—to stress the obvious—a different cast of intellect and creative sensibility from a Ralph Ellison's, a Sonia Sanchez's, a Richard Wright's, an Amiri Baraka's, or an Ed Bullins'. He was, till the end, too deeply fascinated by the ambiguities of moral choices in human relations to posit them in raw conflict terms. His penetrating eyes saw the oppressor as *also* the oppressed. Hate as a revelation of self-hatred, never un-ambiguously outward-directed. Contempt as thwarted love, yearning for expression. Violence as inner fear, insecurity. Cruelty as an inward-turned knife. His was an optimistic, grey-toned vision of humanity in which the domain of mob law and lynch culture is turned inside out to reveal a landscape of scarecrows, an inner content of straws that await the compassionate breath of human love.

LYNN ORILLA SCOTT

Baldwin's Reception and
the Challenge of His Legacy

I.

When James Baldwin died in 1987, five thousand people attended his
funeral at the Cathedral of St. John the Divine in Harlem. The people
came to celebrate his life and to mourn his passing because he had
changed their lives; he was "quite possibly for his times their most
essential interpreter."[1] Literary agent Marie Brown described Baldwin's
passing as "the end of an era." He was "the last survivor ... of those few
most powerful moral articulators who could effectively lecture the
society, among the very few whom we could quote almost daily as
scripture of social consciousness."[2] A substantial number of leading
American writers, intellectuals, and musicians came to pay tribute to
Baldwin. Maya Angelou, Toni Morrison, and Amiri Baraka each gave
eulogies, and many more wrote tributes to Baldwin's life and work that
were published in newspapers around the world, some later in Quincy
Troupe's *James Baldwin: The Legacy* and other venues. In her funeral
address Toni Morrison said that Baldwin, like the Magi, had given her
three gifts: a language to dwell in, the courage to transform the
distances between people into intimacy, and the tenderness of
vulnerability:

From *James Baldwin's Later Fiction: Witness to the Journey.* Pp. 2–18, 177–181. © 2002 by
Lynn Orilla Scott. Reprinted by permission of the author.

No one possessed or inhabited language for me the way you did. You made American English honest—genuinely international. You exposed its secrets and reshaped it until it was truly modern dialogic, representative, humane. You stripped it of ease and false comfort and fake innocence and evasion and hypocrisy. And in place of deviousness was clarity. In place of soft plump lies was a lean, targeted power. In place of intellectual disingenuousness and what you called "exasperating egocentricity," you gave us undecorated truth. You replaced lumbering platitudes with an upright elegance. You went into that forbidden territory and decolonized it, "robbed it of the jewel of its naivete," and un-gated it for black people so that in your wake we could enter it, occupy it, restructure it in order to accommodate our complicated passion—not our vanities but our intricate, difficult, demanding beauty, our tragic, insistent knowledge, our lived reality, our sleek classical imagination—all the while refusing "to be defined by a language that has never been able to recognize [us]." In your hands language was handsome again. In your hands we saw how it was meant to be: neither bloodless nor bloody, and yet alive.[3]

Baldwin's funeral was a dramatic testament of his influence as a writer, thinker, friend, and social activist for the generation that followed him.

However, this funeral service, especially in its omissions, suggests the difficulties of interpreting Baldwin's legacy. Writing for the *Gay Community News*, Barbara Smith said: "Although Baldwin's funeral completely reinforced our Blackness, it tragically rendered his and our homosexuality completely invisible. In those two hours of remembrance and praise, not a syllable was breathed that this wonderful brother, this writer, this warrior, was also gay, that his being gay was indeed integral to his magnificence."[4] Baldwin wrote against a dominant strain of black nationalist thought which placed homosexuality in opposition to black resistance, an ideology that regarded homosexuality as a product of white oppression and evidence of internalized self-hatred. Given the homophobic climate, it is not surprising that interpretations of Baldwin's work that stress his contribution to representing black experience have, until quite recently, ignored or denied the importance of his homosexual themes and the homosexuality of his subjects, as if it were not possible to read his texts as expressions of both black and homosexual experience.[5]

Baldwin also wrote against an ideology that reified racial categories, insisting that "white" and "black" were inventions that oppressed blacks but also imprisoned whites in a false innocence that denied them self knowledge. The only speaker at Baldwin's funeral who was not an African American was the French ambassador. Clyde Taylor found the irony inescapable: "Jimmy, like so many black artists, had been more fully honored and respected abroad than by his own society. France had given him its highest tribute, the Legion of Honor. By contrast, what had American society done?"[6] Perhaps the absence of an official honor from a representative of the American government was, finally, a testament to Baldwin's willingness to sharply criticize American institutions, and to his determination to be among the true poets who are "disturbers of the peace." Yet the absence of any American speaker of European descent is striking, given Baldwin's many white American friends and associates and the considerable impact Baldwin's writing had on the ways white Americans as well as black Americans think about race and sexuality.

Baldwin wrote that as a young man he left America in order to "prevent [himself] from becoming merely a Negro; or, even merely a Negro writer. [He] wanted to find out in what way the specialness of [his] experience could be made to connect [him] with other people instead of dividing [him] from them."[7] Later Baldwin would come to accept, even embrace, the designation of black writer and the enormous responsibility that went with it as part of the historical contingency within which he lived and worked. However, Baldwin never stopped exploring the "specialness" of his experience as it connected him to others. As an American, an African American, and a homosexual, Baldwin sought to provide a witness to overlapping but frequently incompatible experiences and communities. The challenge for writers who interpret his legacy is to find a language that doesn't reduce the complexity of Baldwin's art and vision. As Toni Morrison said in her funeral address: "The difficulty is your life refuses summation—it always did."[8]

At first glance it would seem that James Baldwin's life and work have received considerable attention. To date there have been eight biographies of Baldwin (four of which are for young readers);[9] eight book-length studies of Baldwin's work;[10] eight collections of critical essays; and three collections of tributes written shortly after Baldwin's death.[11] There has been significant bibliographic work done on Baldwin as well.[12] However, it becomes very clear after reviewing the critical output that comparatively little has been written on Baldwin's last three novels. The large majority of criticism has taken one or more of the first three novels as its focus or to a lesser extent the early essays through *The Fire Next Time*. Of the full-length studies only Carolyn Wedin Sylvander's discusses all of Baldwin's novels, and her book is primarily a reader's guide. Horace Porter's *Stealing the Fire* (1989) explores the influence of Henry James, Harriet Beecher Stowe, and Richard Wright on Baldwin's early essays and fiction, dismissing Baldwin's work after *The Fire Next Time* as unsuccessful. Porter's book is the most recent of the full-length critical studies (not including Bobia's book on Baldwin's reception in France), yet it is over ten years old. Trudier Harris's *Black Women in the Fiction of James Baldwin* (1985) provides close readings of *If Beale Street Could Talk* and *Just Above My Head* but omits any discussion of *Tell Me How Long the Train's Been Gone* since it has no major black women characters. Macebuh's, Möller's, and Pratt's studies were written prior to the publication of Baldwin's last novel or novels.

The critical collections have emphasized Baldwin's earlier work as well. Even D. Quentin Miller's recent *Re-viewing James Baldwin: Things Not Seen* (1999), which purports to give attention to Baldwin's neglected later work, has no discussion of *Tell Me How Long the Train's Been Gone* or *If Beale Street Could Talk* and only one essay on *Just Above My Head*. Miller's collection does, however, include important work on some of Baldwin's lesser-known writing, some of which was written during the seventies and eighties.[13] A number of the contributors to Dwight McBride's *James Baldwin Now* see Baldwin's work as a progenitor to theoretical developments in gender and gay studies as well as to the study of the cultural construction of whiteness. These essays, on the whole, do a much more sophisticated job of analyzing Baldwin's work as it complicates and interimplicates categories of race, gender, and sexuality than early essays were able to do.[14] They replace the old image of the fifties Baldwin as a liberal humanist with a much more complex figure, one who intervened in, rather than merely reflected, the liberal discourse of the period. However, the focus of this collection is Baldwin's early work, particularly *Giovanni's Room* and *Another Country*, in the context of post–World War II American culture. As a result there is little discussion of Baldwin's response to the changing culture and conditions of the sixties and seventies, and there is little discussion of Baldwin's representations of black families and of black communities, since there is nothing on *Go Tell It on the Mountain*, *Tell Me How Long the Train's Been Gone*, *If Beale Street Could Talk*, or *Just Above My Head*.[15]

In her introduction to *Black Women in the Fiction of James Baldwin* (1985), Trudier Harris wrote that she was "surprised to discover that a writer of Baldwin's reputation evoked such vague memories from individuals in the scholarly community" and found it "discouraging ... that one of America's best-known writers, and certainly one of its best-known black writers, has not attained a more substantial place in the scholarship on Afro-American writers."[16] Although there was renewed interest in Baldwin's life and work in the late eighties following his death (as evidenced by the publication of James Campbell's and David Leeming's biographies, Quincy Troupe's *James Baldwin: The Legacy*, the published proceedings of a conference at the University of Massachusetts at Amherst, and the film *The Price of the Ticket*), the quantity of scholarship on Baldwin's writing has significantly lagged behind that of other well-known African American writers, such as Richard Wright, Ralph Ellison, or Toni Morrison. Moreover, Baldwin studies have not benefited from the presence of African American theory and scholarship in the academy. Craig Werner pointed out the extent to which Baldwin has been ignored:

> To be sure, Baldwin's name is occasionally invoked, generally as part of a trinity including Richard Wright and Ralph Ellison. But his work, much less his vision, is rarely discussed, even within the field of Afro-American Studies. Baldwin is conspicuous by his absence from recent (and valuable) books on cultural theory (Henry Louis Gates Jr.'s *The Signifying Monkey*, Robert Stepto's *From Behind the Veil*, Houston Baker's *Blues, Ideology, and Afro-American Literature: A Vernacular Theory*); intellectual history (Sterling Stuckey's *Slave Culture: Nationalist Theory and the Foundations of Black America*, Harold Cruse's *Plural But Equal: Black and Minorities in America's Plural Society*); literary criticism (Keith Byerman's *Fingering the Jagged*

Grain: Tradition and Form in Recent Black Fiction, John Callahan's *In the African-American Grain: The Pursuit of Voice in Twentieth-Century Black Fiction*); and period history (David Garrow's *Bearing the Cross*, Doug McAdam's *Freedom Summer*). There are to be sure occasional exceptions, mostly [sic] notably Michael Cooke's *Afro-American Literature in the Twentieth Century* and Melvin Dixon's *Ride Out the Wilderness: Geography and Identity in Afro-American Literature*. Still, given Baldwin's central importance to the development of issues raised in all of the above work, the general silence suggests that the larger changes of intellectual fashion have influenced the internal dynamics of discourse on Afro-American culture.[17]

Werner attributes Baldwin's marginalization in the academy to the dominance of a poststructuralist critique which "resurrected an ironic sensibility that renders Baldwin's moral seriousness and his political activism nearly incomprehensible to literary intellectuals."[18] While Baldwin's "concern with salvation" may have made him unfashionable, his incisive critique of racial and sexual categories in the formation of American identity certainly precede the poststructuralist critique of "identity." Eric Savoy has pointed out the limitation of a great deal of criticism that argues that Baldwin's main theme is "a search for identity." The direction of Baldwin's work is not toward the attainment of identity, but rather toward knowledge of self "as implicated, situated subject, but simultaneously as 'other' and therefore as resisting agent."[19] Baldwin's neglect by the academy may be explained by the dominance of an intellectual sensibility that rendered political activism and moral seriousness incomprehensible, as Werner claims. However, Baldwin's marginalization is also partly due to the pressures of canonizing black literature by defining a black difference. Baldwin's critique of racial representation—what Savoy has called his "double resistance" to both white, middle-class, heterosexual America and to the ways in which other black writers (especially Richard Wright) and gay writers (Andre Gide) brought their otherness to text—puts Baldwin at odds with at least some theories of black difference.

In Houston A. Baker Jr.'s influential *Blues, Ideology, and Afro-American Literature: A Vernacular Theory*, as well as in his earlier book *The Journey Back: Issues in Black Literature and Criticism*, Baldwin is not exactly ignored. He becomes the "other" in Baker's attempt to canonize Richard Wright as the writer whose work best reveals a distinctive and resistant African American discourse. Baker defends Wright from the negative critique of *Native Son* and of "protest fiction" in Baldwin's "Everybody's Protest Novel" and "Many Thousands Gone." According to Baker, Baldwin's criticism of Wright is based on a bourgeois aesthetic in which the artist is perceived to be above or separate from society.[20] While Baker's deconstruction of the binary "art" versus "protest" is useful in revealing the political motivation of 1950s "aesthetic" criticism, he reinstates the binary by portraying Wright as the black writer with a political consciousness and Baldwin as the writer who advocates "a theology of art," whose writing is "poetic, analytical, asocial."[21] However, Baldwin's criticism of *Native Son* was as much politically motivated as it was aesthetically motivated. His argument with Wright turned less on artistic flaws in the depiction of Bigger Thomas than on a racist representation of the black male in which Baldwin believed the novel to be implicated.[22]

One of the central problems of Baldwin's reception has been the way in which arguments over "art" and "politics" have misrepresented and marginalized his work. Baker's characterization of the difference between Wright and Baldwin mirrors and reverses the response of those New Critics who embraced Baldwin's criticism of Wright and read Baldwin's first novel as a vindication of their literary values, which emphasized formal structures over social criticism. Yet as Horace Porter, Craig Werner, and others have argued, Baldwin's early work, including *Go Tell It on the Mountain*, was not apolitical. As Werner points out, "Just as the original readers of *Native Son* simplified the work to accommodate their ideology, Baldwin's aesthetic defenders ignored major political elements of his novel."[23] Horace Porter's book (appropriately subtitled *The Art and Politics of James Baldwin*) makes this argument in detail by elaborating the intertexuality in Baldwin's early work with both Wright and Stowe.

While Baldwin has been criticized by some Marxist and some African American literary theorists for his alleged bourgeois aesthetics, with the publication of *Blues for Mister Charlie*, *Tell Me How Long the Train's Been Gone*, *No Name in the Street*, and *If Beale Street Could Talk* Baldwin came under attack in the liberal press by Mario Puzo, Pearl K. Bell, John Aldridge, and others for writing "propaganda." Using Baldwin's early statements on protest fiction against him, they argued

that Baldwin was doing the very thing for which he had criticized
Richard Wright: he was writing protest fiction with melodramatic plots
and stereotypical characters. Moreover, taking offense at the occasional
use of "street" language and the sharper, more militant tone, many of
these critics argued that Baldwin's "bitterness" revealed that he was out
of touch with American "progress" in race relations. Those who had
embraced Baldwin's early work for aesthetic reasons felt betrayed.

To a large extent the scholarly community has agreed with the
initial assessment of Baldwin's later novels. Horace Porter found
Baldwin's later essays and fiction deeply disappointing:

> he moves from the promethean figure, the man who stole the
> fire of "Notes of a Native Son," the powerful writer of *The
> Fire Next Time*, to the embittered and self-indulgent nay-
> sayer of *No Name in the Street* and *Evidence of Things Not Seen*.
> None of Baldwin's later novels or essays rivals the narrative
> ingenuity and rhetorical power of *Go Tell It on the Mountain*
> and *Notes of a Native Son*, his first novel and his first
> collection of essays.[24]

Henry Louis Gates Jr. and Hilton Als concur with this evaluation
of Baldwin's decline as an artist and place the blame on black militants
(most notably Eldridge Cleaver), from whose criticism Baldwin allegedly
never recovered. Gates views *No Name in the Street*, in particular, as a
"capitulation" by a man who was desperate "to be loved by his own" and
who "cared too much about what others wanted from him."[25] Reviewing
the 1998 Library of America's two-volume selection of Baldwin's essays,
early novels, and stories, Hilton Als reflects on "both [his] early
infatuation and [his] later disaffection" with Baldwin's work. Because
Baldwin "compromised" his unique perspective and "sacrificed his gifts
to gain acceptance from the Black Power movement," Als sees Baldwin's
career as "a cautionary tale ... a warning as well as an inspiration."[26]

Clearly Baldwin has been in the crossfire of arguments that
assume certain artistic and social values and set them in
contradistinction. In fact, it remains very difficult to sort out aesthetic
from political judgments when discussing Baldwin's reception because
they are so deeply interconnected. One of the aims of this book is to
interrogate the assumption that Baldwin's increased political activism
and militancy in the sixties led to his decline as an artist. The reading of

Baldwin's later work as lacking aesthetic value is as problematic as the reading of his earlier work as lacking political value. As Craig Werner has pointed out, James Baldwin "asserted the ultimately moral connection of political and cultural experience."[27] There is no doubt that Baldwin's later work was influenced by the turbulent political and racial environment of the sixties and early seventies, as well as by the decline in economic and social conditions for urban black youth and families in the seventies. I wish to argue that his response to the events of the sixties and seventies was more complex than has been acknowledged and that his last three novels should be read not as evidence of either a political capitulation or an artistic decline, but as evidence of the ways Baldwin creatively responded to a changing racial environment and discourse in an attempt to communicate the story he wanted to tell.

As the only major African American writer whose career spanned the pre– and post–civil rights and black power period, Baldwin's historical position was unique. Richard Wright died in 1960; Langston Hughes died in 1967; Ralph Ellison survived Baldwin, but stopped writing (or at least publishing) fiction. The sensibilities of prominent contemporary African American writers, including Toni Morrison, Alice Walker, and Amiri Baraka, were formed in the crucible of the civil rights era. Baldwin's work from the middle sixties on reflected the dramatic shift in American racial and political discourse, symbolized by the positive signification of "black" and the deployment of a resistant identity politics. His work also reflected a racial and political reality that Baldwin read as increasingly repressive, even genocidal, for the majority of black Americans, a reading that put him at sharp odds with a liberal rhetoric of black progress.

Tell Me How Long the Train's Been Gone, *If Beale Street Could Talk*, and *Just Above My Head* are not flawless novels. There are some overwritten, even carelessly written passages and some inconsistencies in character and plot that are difficult to account for and that could have been corrected by more careful editing. Yet to focus solely on artistic faults (which the majority of reviewers did) is to ignore the power and vision present in these works. Moreover, what some reviewers described as artistic flaws were certainly aspects of Baldwin's intentional experimentation with voice and form. Baldwin took risks with his later work. He reframed his earlier stories to reflect his experience and, especially, his interest in reproducing in the novel a style of resistance that he found in African American music. Baldwin gave up the tighter, more formal structures of his earliest work. For example, the compartmentalized and isolated voices of the characters in *Go Tell It on the Mountain* give way to experiments in first-person narration. These novels demonstrate a relationship between author and character (i.e., Baldwin's relationship to Leo Proudhammer, Tish Rivers, and Hall Montana) that parallels a jazz musician's relationship to his instrument as an extension or elaboration of the performer's self.[28] Baldwin's narrators are instruments of self-expression who perform Baldwin's voice in different bodies—both male and female—and in different places— Harlem, the Village, Paris. They echo and revise the author's life. They suggest that "identity" is, indeed, a complex affair that involves a recognition of "others" and the presence of the "other" in.the "self."

II.

In 1988, shortly after Baldwin's death, a conference at the University of Massachusetts at Amherst brought several eminent writers and scholars together to pay tribute to James Baldwin. The published proceedings of this conference gave voice to a deep concern with the type of criticism Baldwin had been receiving. Describing literary criticism as an open letter to an author, John Edgar Wideman said, "We're getting a species of letter which endangers my relationship to James Baldwin and James Baldwin's relationship to the tradition and to you and to your children." In these "poison-pen letters," Baldwin is cast as "a kind of villain" who "does not appreciate progress. He is enraged and bitter. He lost his footing as an artist and simply became a propagandist. And that version of Baldwin's career is very dangerously being promulgated and it's being pushed in a kind of surreptitious way by these letters."[29] Chinua Achebe sought to clarify Baldwin's accomplishment. Responding to the frequent charge that Baldwin failed to recognize America's progress, Achebe pointed out that for Baldwin progress was not a matter of more black mayors and generals. Baldwin's project was to "redefine the struggle" by seeing it "from a whole range of perspectives at once—the historical, the psychological, the philosophical, which are not present in a handful of statistics of recent advances." Baldwin's strength was in his ability "to lift from the backs of Black people the burden of their race" and "to unmask the face of the oppressor, to see his face and to call him by name." Achebe concluded that "Baldwin, belongs to mankind's ancient tradition of storytelling, to the tradition of prophets who had the dual role to fore-tell and to forth-tell."[30]

Although the proceedings of the Amherst conference offer a corrective to the white liberal dismissal of Baldwin's work after the middle sixties, they completely ignore Baldwin's homosexual themes and, more important, the extent to which black and white homophobia affected Baldwin's reception. There was more than one version of the "poison-pen letter." Around the same time Baldwin was being condemned by white liberals for his black militancy, he was being condemned by black militants for his homosexuality. The most notorious example was Eldridge Cleaver's attack on Baldwin in *Soul on Ice*: "There is in James Baldwin's work the most grueling, agonizing, total hatred of the blacks, particularly of himself, and the most shameful, fanatical, fawning, sycophantic love of the whites that one can find in the writings of any black American writer of note in our time."[31]

Cleaver argues that there is a "decisive quirk" in Baldwin's writing that caused him to "slander Rufus Scott in *Another Country*, venerate Andre Gide, repudiate [Norman Mailer's] *The White Negro*, and drive the blade of Brutus into the corpse of Richard Wright."[32] Charging Baldwin with waging "a despicable underground guerrilla war ... against black masculinity" and calling "homosexuality a sickness, just as are baby-rape or wanting to become the head of General Motors,"[33] Cleaver expresses in virulent form a homophobia representative of some segments of the black community.

In Cleaver's analysis, which parallels that of conservative black critics such as Stanley Crouch, homosexuality is considered to be a remnant of slavery, a habit learned from whites and thus a symptom of internalized self-hatred. In this reading Baldwin's homosexuality necessarily negates any claim that Baldwin can speak to an authentic "black" experience. Of course homophobic responses to Baldwin's work are not limited to black critics. In writing about *Another Country*, Robert Bone said:

Few will concede to a sense of reality, at least in the sexual realm, to one who regards heterosexual love as "a kind of superior calisthenics." To most, homosexuality will seem rather an evasion than an affirmation of human truth. Ostensibly the novel summons us to reality. Actually it

substitutes for the illusions of white supremacy those of
homosexual love.[34]

Although not exactly the same argument as Cleaver's, Bone's
argument also links homosexuality with white supremacy as a travesty of
truth. Numerous critics took the position that Baldwin's representations
of bisexuality and homosexuality undermined his credibility as a novelist
and as a spokesperson for blacks. In addition Baldwin's sexuality put him
in a difficult relationship to other civil rights leaders; it was probably the
main reason he was not invited to speak at the 1963 March on
Washington.[35]

Emmanuel S. Nelson has effectively documented the homophobia
in Baldwin's reception, in its silences as well as in its more obvious forms,
and has suggested that the reason Baldwin has been more highly
regarded as an essayist than as a novelist is related to the relative absence
of homosexual themes in his essays compared with his novels.[36]
Homophobia may also be at the center of the decline in Baldwin's
reputation as a novelist since his later novels, with the exception of *If
Beale Street Could Talk*, are increasingly positive and explicit in their
representation of black homosexual relationships. Given this fact, the
belief that Baldwin adapted his writing or "compromised" his vision to
please critics such as Cleaver seems unfounded. In the face of black
homophobia Baldwin responded by continuing to represent and even
celebrate homosexuality in *Tell Me How Long the Train's Been Gone* and
Just Above My Head. Nelson calls for an analysis of Baldwin's work that
explores both his "racial awareness and his homosexual consciousness on
his literary imagination" without privileging one over the other.[37] Bryan
R. Washington expresses caution over "politically fashionable" but
hollow efforts to "recanonize" Baldwin by avoiding his "homopoetics
(politics)." He argues that such avoidance "proceeds from a desire to
keep the recanonizing train on track—a train driven by theories of race
and writing designed to minimize difference, to promote the academic
institutionalization of blackness by homogenizing it."[38]

Although Baldwin has been underrepresented in the field of
African American studies compared to other black writers of his
stature, he has received substantial treatment in many studies on gay
male writing, including Georges-Michel Sarotte's *Like a Brother, Like a
Lover* (1976, translated into English, 1978), Stephen Adams's *The
Homosexual as Hero in Contemporary Fiction* (1980), Claude J. Summers's

Gay Fictions: Wilde to Stonewall (1990), David Bergman's *Gaiety Transfigured: Gay Self-Representation in America* (1991), Mark Lilly's *Gay Men's Literature in the Twentieth Century* (1993), and Wilfrid R. Koponen's *Embracing a Gay Identity: Gay Novels as Guides* (1993). Yet all of these studies ignore Baldwin's later fiction (and only Sarotte's book was published before Baldwin's last novel). None discuss *Just Above My Head*, and *Tell Me How Long the Train's Been Gone* receives only passing mention, if any at all. Summers and Koponen work strictly with *Giovanni's Room*, while Adams and Lilly work with both *Giovanni's Room* and *Another Country*.

In his substantial chapter on Baldwin, Stephen Adams argues that "the knowledge Baldwin claims of American masculinity—as one who has been menaced by it—has an authority which in turn menaces preferred images of manhood, both black and white. He puzzles over his own definitions in ways which explode the notions of narrowness in the experience of a racial or sexual minority."[39] Adams takes several of Baldwin's critics to task, including Irving Howe, who charges Baldwin with "whipped cream sentimentalism" in the portrayal of homosexual love in *Giovanni's Room*, and Sarotte, who reads *Giovanni's Room* as memoir and identifies David's position as a homophobic homophile with Baldwin's. While Adams develops careful and sympathetic readings of *Giovanni's Room* and *Another Country*, he dismisses *Tell Me How Long the Train's Been Gone* in the last paragraph, calling it Baldwin's endorsement of black militancy and describing the Leo–Christopher relationship as a product of Baldwin's "wishful thinking" that "rings false."[40] David Bergman's treatment of Baldwin occurs within a broad discussion of black discourse on racism and sexuality, evangelical Protestantism, Africa as racial homeland, and the coded discourse of earlier black homosexual writers, especially Alain Locke. What could be a promising approach to the intersection of race and homosexuality in Baldwin's writing is marred by Bergman's uninformed statements about Baldwin's work. For example, Bergman is seemingly unaware of Baldwin's theoretical and personal essays on homosexuality—"The Preservation of Innocence" and "There Be Dragons"—when he claims that Baldwin's only nonfiction on homosexuality is "The Male Prison."[41] In addition, Bergman's assertion that "after Cleaver's attack, Baldwin emphasized racial much more than sexual issues" is simply not supported by Baldwin's later work.[42]

That most gay studies ignore Baldwin's later novels adds weight to

Nelson's observation that analyses which privilege Baldwin's homosexuality tend to ignore his blackness. Unlike *Giovanni's Room* and *Another Country*, the homosexuality of *Tell Me How Long the Train's Been Gone* and of *Just Above My Head* occurs within a specifically black context, making it impossible to explore the representation of homosexuality in these novels without also. addressing the representation of race. Melvin Dixon's chapter on Baldwin in *Ride out the Wilderness* and Lee Edelman's essay, "The Part for the (W)hole: Baldwin, Homophobia, and the Fantasmatics of 'Race,'" in *Homographesis* are important exceptions to the tendency to privilege either "blackness" or "homosexuality" when reading Baldwin's texts, and both produce very interesting, although quite different, readings of *Just Above My Head*.[43]

In the history of twentieth-century American letters it would be hard to find another figure more simultaneously praised and damned, often by the same critic in the same essay, than James Baldwin. A remarkable aspect of Cleaver's response to Baldwin is its initial adulation of Baldwin's work and the way this adulation is expressed in clearly sexual terms. From the beginning tone of Cleaver's essay, one would not expect the coming attack. Cleaver describes the "continuous delight" he felt reading "a couple of James Baldwin's books." He describes Baldwin's talent as "penetrating" and says he "lusted for anything Baldwin had written. It would have been a gas for [him] to sit on a pillow beneath the womb of Baldwin's typewriter and catch each newborn page as it entered this world of ours."[44] However, Cleaver begins to feel "an aversion in [his] heart to part of the song [Baldwin] sang" and after reading *Another Country* he "knew why [his] love for Baldwin's vision had become ambivalent."[45] This movement from praise and identification with Baldwin's work to ambivalence, disappointment, and rejection is the single most common characteristic of Baldwin criticism, regardless of the particular ideological, racial, or sexual orientation of the critic. (Noting the irony, Craig Werner has pointed out that "it is perhaps not surprising that Baldwin's blackness has never been clearer than in his rejection."[46])

Baldwin's work has presented problems to readers from almost every perspective—liberal, black nationalist, feminist, and homosexual—and to some extent each of these constituencies in their inability to accommodate Baldwin's complexity has helped to marginalize him. In addition to the previously discussed challenges he presents to both liberal and nationalist discourses, Baldwin's work gets an ambivalent response from feminist and gay criticism as well. Although Baldwin's female characters are numerous, varied, and complex, especially when compared to other black male writers of his generation, Trudier Harris, Hortense Spillers, and others have critiqued Baldwin's discourse for essentializing gender, and his female characters for their dependence on men and male values. While acknowledging Baldwin's tremendous contribution to making the representation of a gay black male sexuality possible, some pro-gay critics are uncomfortable with Baldwin's reluctance to discuss gay issues in his nonfiction or to assert a gay identity. (Baldwin insisted that "homosexual" was not a noun.) The predominance of bisexual characters in Baldwin's fiction and his use of a heterosexual narrator to describe homosexual experience in *Just Above My Head* is taken by some as evidence of the extent to which Baldwin is, himself, implicated by the homophobia he so trenchantly critiques.

What these narratives of disappointment suggest is that James Baldwin did not tell the story that various critical constituencies wanted him to tell. For the white liberal he did not confirm that the "success" of a talented black individual represented the "progress" of the race; for black and white integrationists he seemed to lose faith in the dream of interracial understanding; for the black nationalist his stories did not evoke masculine-individualist heroics (and thus were judged as stories of complicity rather than resistance); for the feminist his women characters were too traditional in their relationships to men, and his concern with reinventing "masculinity" appeared to construct the feminine as other; for the gay activist he did not assert a separate homosexual identity. The critical narratives of Baldwin's "unfulfilled potential" must be understood in terms of the critics' own desire for a particular kind of spokesperson, but they also must be understood in relationship to the "promise" that Baldwin presents to his readership and to his politics of "salvation." (As Baldwin said in a 1987 interview, "I am working toward the New Jerusalem. That's true. I'm not joking. I won't live to see it but I do believe in it. I think we're going to be better than we are."[47]) While Baldwin's concern for salvation may make him incomprehensible to a certain poststructuralist sensibility, as Werner claims, it also raises expectations in readers who would probably not agree on just what the New Jerusalem should look like. Baldwin did not leave a map of his heavenly city, only a few trail markers to indicate the way.

Baldwin's work is wedded to the tradition of realistic fiction as well as to the tradition of the jeremiad, which seeks to call people to their better selves while warning them of the failings and the dangers of their current course. His work is driven by two traditions, which are not always compatible: the tradition of mimetic truth telling and the tradition of religious truth telling. The first called Baldwin to testify to the sorrows, joys, contingencies, and interruptions of everyday experience, while the second called him to exhort, to promise, and to create a vision of a new and better order out of the old, corrupt one. It is the balance Baldwin creates between these two impulses that make up his distinctive voice. His fidelity to lived experience and to representing human relationships in all their complexity signifies on what Baldwin called "the protest novel." His commitment to a moral vision also signifies on "the protest novel," requiring that he, too, protest, but in a different key.

NOTES

1. Clyde Taylor, "Celebrating Jimmy," in *James Baldwin: The Legacy*, ed. Quincy Troupe (New York: Touchstone-Simon and Schuster, 1989), 30.

2. Ibid., 37.

3. Toni Morrison, "Life in His Language," in *James Baldwin: The Legacy*, 76.

4. Barbara Smith, "We Must Always Bury Our Dead Twice," *Gay Community News*, 20–26 December 1987: center and 10.

5. Patricia Holland addresses the way in which discursive boundaries have made the black gay subject invisible: "The disciplines of feminist, lesbian-gay, and African American studies have imagined for themselves appropriate subjects to be removed, at least theoretically, from such a contentious space into the place of recognition. These bodies/subjects are either white but not heterosexual or black but not homosexual. In the crack between discourses, the black and queer subject resides." See "(Pro)Creating Imaginative Spaces and Other Queer Acts," in *James Baldwin Now*, ed. Dwight McBride (New York: New York University Press, 1999), 266.

6. Taylor, "Celebrating Jimmy," 33–34.

7. James Baldwin, "The Discovery of What It Means to Be an American," in *The Price of the Ticket: Collected Nonfiction, 1948–1985* (New York: St. Martin's and Marek, 1985), 171.

8. Morrison, "Life in His Language," 75.

9. Biographies of James Baldwin include David Leeming, *James Baldwin: A Biography* (New York: Alfred A. Knopf, 1994); James Campbell, *Talking at the Gates: A Life of James Baldwin* (New York: Penguin, 1991); W.J. Weatherby, *James Baldwin: Artist on Fire* (New York: Dell, 1989); and Fern Marja Eckman, *The Furious Passage of James Baldwin* (New York: M. Evans, 1966). Juvenile biographies include Lisa Rosser, *James Baldwin* (New York: Chelsea House, 1989); Randall Kenan, *James Baldwin* (New York: Chelsea House, 1994); Ted Gottfried, *James Baldwin: Voice from Harlem* (New York: E Watts, 1997); and James Tachach, *James Baldwin* (San Diego: Lucent Books, 1997).

10. Single author, book-length studies that focus solely on Baldwin's work include Rosa Bobia, *The Critical Reception of James Baldwin in France* (New York: Peter Lang, 1997); Horace Porter, *Stealing the Fire: The Art and Protest of James Baldwin* (Middletown, Conn.: Wesleyan University Press, 1989); Trudier Harris, *Black Women in the Fiction of James Baldwin* (Knoxville, Tenn.: University of Tennessee Press, 1985); Carolyn Wedin Sylvander, *James Baldwin* (New York: Frederick Ungar, 1980); Louis H. Pratt, *James Baldwin* (Boston: Twayne Publishers, 1978); and Stanley Macebuh, *James Baldwin: A Critical Study* (New York: Third Press, 1973). European monographs on Baldwin's work include Karin Möller, *The Theme of Identity in the Essays of James Baldwin: An Interpretation* (Goteborg, Sweden: Acta Universitatis Gothoburgensis, 1975); and Peter Bruck, *Von der "Storefront Church" zum "American Dream": James Baldwin und der amerikanische Rassenkonflikt* (Amsterdam: n.p., 1975).

11. Edited collections of critical essays on Baldwin's work include D. Quentin Miller, ed., *Re-viewing James Baldwin: Things Not Seen* (Philadelphia: Temple University Press, 2000); Dwight A. McBride, ed., *James Baldwin Now* (New York: New York University Press, 1999); Trudier Harris, ed., *New Essays on "Go Tell It on the Mountain"* (New York: Cambridge University Press, 1999); Jakob Kollhofer, ed., *James Baldwin: His Place in American Literary History and His Reception in Europe* (New York: Peter Lang, 1991); Fred L. Standley and Nancy V. Burt, ed., *Critical Essays on James Baldwin* (Boston: G. K. Hall, 1988); Harold Bloom, ed., *James Baldwin* (New York: Chelsea House Publishers, 1986); Therman B. O'Daniel, ed., *James Baldwin: A Critical Evaluation* (Washington, D.C.: Howard University Press, 1977); and Kenneth

Kinnamon, ed., *James Baldwin: A Collection of Critical Essays* (Englewood Cliffs, N.J.: Prentice-Hall, 1974). Tributes to James Baldwin include Quincy Troupe, ed., *James Baldwin: The Legacy* (New York: Touchstone-Simon and Schuster, 1989); Jules Chametzky, ed., *Black Writers Redefine the Struggle: A Tribute to James Baldwin* (Amherst, Mass.: University of Massachusetts Press, 1989); and Ralph Reckley, ed., *James Baldwin in Memoriam: Proceedings of the Annual Conference of the Middle Atlantic Writers' Association*, 1989 (Baltimore: Middle Atlantic Writers' Association Press, 1992).

12. For the most complete listing of Baldwin's published work, see David Leeming and Lisa Gitelman's "Chronological Bibliography of Printed Works by James Baldwin," in David Leeming's *James Baldwin*, 405–17. To get a picture of the initial reception of Baldwin's work through *If Beale Street Could Talk* and the first three decades of critical response, see Fred L. Standley and Nancy V. Standley's *James Baldwin: A Reference Guide* (Boston: G.K. Hall, 1980), which provides an annotated bibliography of writings about James Baldwin from 1946 to 1978. Also see Daryl Dance's "James Baldwin," in *Black American Writers Bibliographical Essays*, vol. 2, ed. Thomas Inge et al. (New York: St. Martin's, 1978), 73–119. While no one has matched the thoroughness of the Standleys' *Reference Guide*, there have been subsequent bibliographic lists and essays, including the introduction to Fred L. Standley and Nancy V. Burt's *Critical Essays on James Baldwin*; and Jeffrey W. Hole, "Select Bibliography of Works by and on James Baldwin," in *James Baldwin Now*, 393–409. Among other things, Hole lists seventy-five essays published on the work of James Baldwin between 1985 and 1997 and thirty-eight dissertations that include a significant discussion of Baldwin's work published during the same years.

13. See, for example, Cassandra M. Ellis, "The Black Boy Looks at the Silver Screen: Baldwin as Moviegoer," in *Re-viewing James Baldwin*, 190–214; and D. Quentin Miller, "James Baldwin, Poet," in *Re-viewing James Baldwin*, 233–54.

14. See, for example, Yasmin Y. DeGout, "'Masculinity' and (Im)maturity: 'The Man Child' and Other Stories in Baldwin's Gender Studies Enterprise," in *Re-viewing James Baldwin*, 134. De Gout argues that "any reading of Baldwin's fiction reveals him to be progenitor of many of the theoretical formulations currently. associated with feminist, gay, and gender studies.... Baldwin ultimately reveals in his fiction how sexism and heterosexism affect women and men in a gendered society

and how gender constructs are inseparably linked to race, class, and other identity categories."

15. An exception to the focus on Baldwin's earlier work is Nicholas Boggs, "Of Mimicry and (Little Man Little) Man: Toward a Queer Sighted Theory of Black Childhood," in *James Baldwin Flow*, 122–60. Boggs reads Baldwin's 1976 *Little Man Little Man: A Story of Childhood* in the contexts of metaphors of African Americanist criticism and queer theory.

16. Harris, *Black Women in the Fiction of James Baldwin*, 3–4.

17. Craig Werner, "James Baldwin: Politics and the Gospel Impulse," *New Politics: A Journal of Socialist Thought* 2, no. 2 (1989): 107.

18. Ibid.

19. Eric Savoy, "Other (ed) Americans in Paris: Henry James, James Baldwin, and the Subversion of Identity," *English Studies in Canada* 18, no. 3 (1992): 3.

20. Houston A. Baker Jr., *Blues, Ideology, and Afro-American Literature: A Vernacular Theory* (Chicago: University of Chicago Press, 1984), 140–42.

21. Houston A. Baker Jr., *The Journey Back: Issues in Black Literature and Criticism* (Chicago: University of Chicago Press, 1980), 60–61.

22. Lawrie Balfour has also recently argued that Baldwin's critique of *Native Son* is not "purely an aesthetic one." Baldwin's objection is moral in that he argues the protest novel helps perpetuate what he has called "the myth of innocence." See her essay "Finding the Words: Baldwin, Race Consciousness, and Democratic Theory," in *James Baldwin Now*, 76–77.

23. Werner, "James Baldwin," 111.

24. Porter, *Stealing the Fire*, 160. Houston A. Baker Jr., however, came to the defense of Baldwin's later work. See "The Embattled Craftsman: An Essay on James Baldwin," *The Journal of African-Afro-American Affairs* 1, no. 1 (1977): 28–51, where Baker argues that Baldwin needs a new kind of critic who understands his relationship to African American literature and culture. See the following chapter for further discussion.

25. Henry Louis Gates Jr., "What James Baldwin Can and Can't Teach America," *New Republic*, 1 June 1992, 42.

26. Hilton Als, "The Enemy Within," *The New Yorker*, 16 February 1998, 72, 78. Also see Henry Louis Gates Jr. and Nellie McKay's introduction to Baldwin in *The Norton Anthology of African American*

Literature (New York: W.W. Norton and Co., 1997) for a summary of the negative assessment of Baldwin's later work.

27. Werner, "James Baldwin," 106.

28. In *Blues People: Negro Music in White America* (New York: William Morrow, 1963), 30–31, LeRoi Jones's description of Charlie Parker's relationship to his alto saxophone had great resonance for me as I thought about the relationship between Baldwin and many of the characters he created (especially the four autobiographical characters in *Just Above My Head*, each of whom are named after Baldwin). Jones says, Parker produced a sound that "would literally imitate the human voice with his cries, swoops, squawks, and slurs.... Parker did not admit that there was any separation between himself and the agent he had chosen as his means of self-expression."

29. Chametzky, *Black Writers Redefine the Struggle*, 66.

30. As quoted in ibid., 6–7.

31. Eldridge Cleaver, *Soul on Ice* (New York: Delta-Dell, 1968), 99.

32. Ibid., 105.

33. Ibid., 109–10.

34. Robert Bone as quoted in David Bergman, *Gaiety Transfigured: Gay Self-Representation in American Literature* (Madison: University of Wisconsin Press, 1991), 164–65.

35. David Leeming says that Baldwin knew that "people were wary of his reputation as a homosexual and he was disappointed that he had not been asked to participate [in the March on Washington] in any meaningful way" (*James Baldwin* 228). Lee Edelman deconstructs the barely coded homophobic language that was used to describe Baldwin in *Time Magazine* and in other public arenas, language that marginalized or negated Baldwin's role as a civil rights leader. He points out that such "humorous" descriptions of Baldwin as "Martin Luther Queen" combined racism and homophobia to discredit King and the movement as well as Baldwin. See *Homographesis: Essays in Gay Literary and Cultural Theory* (New York: Routledge, 1994), 42–44.

36. Emmanuel S. Nelson, "Critical Deviance: Homophobia and the Reception of James Baldwin's Fiction," *Journal of American Culture* 14, no. 3 (1991): 91–96.

37. Ibid., 91.

38. Bryan R. Washington, *The Politics of Exile: Ideology in Henry James, F. Scott Fitzgerald, and James Baldwin* (Boston: Northeastern University

Press, 1995), 97. 39. Stephen Adams, *The Homosexual as Hero in Contemporary Fiction* (New York: Harper and Row, 1980), 36.

40. Ibid., 54.

41. Bergman, *Gaiety Transfigured*, 168.

42. Ibid., 166.

43. Melvin Dixon, *Ride out the Wilderness: Geography and Identity in Afro-American Literature* (Urbana: University of Illinois, 1987); Edelman, *Homographesis*.

44. Cleaver, *Soul on Ice*, 97.

45. Ibid., 98

46. Werner, "James Baldwin," 112.

47. James Baldwin, "The Last Interview (1987)," interview with Quincy Troupe, in *James Baldwin: The Legacy*, 184.

C.W.E. BIGSBY

The Divided Mind of James Baldwin

Lionel Trilling once observed that there are certain individuals who contain the "yes" and "no" of their culture, whose personal ambivalences become paradigmatic. This would seem to be an apt description of a man whose first novel was published twenty-five years ago, a man whose career has described a neat and telling parabola and whose contradictions go to the heart of an issue which dominated the political and cultural life of mid-century America: James Baldwin. And it is perhaps not inappropriate to seize the occasion of this anniversary and of the publication of his new novel, *Just Above My Head*, to attempt a summation of a writer, once an articulate spokesman for black revolt, now living an expatriate existence in southern France.

To date, Baldwin has written six novels: *Go Tell it on the Mountain* (1954), *Giovanni's Room* (1956), *Another Country* (1962), *Tell Me How Long the Train's Been Gone* (1968), *If Beale Street Could Talk* (1974), *Just Above My Head* (1979); four books of essays: *The Fire Next Time* (1963), *Nobody Knows My Name* (1964), *Notes of a Native Son* (1964), *No Name in the Street* (1972); two plays: *Blues for Mr. Charlie* (1964), *Amen Corner* (1968); and one book of short stories: *Going to Meet the Man* (1965). Born in Harlem in 1924, he left in 1948 for France, driven out by despair of the racial situation. He returned in 1957 and in the heady days of the Civil Rights movement found himself a principal spokesman—his

From *Critical Essays on James Baldwin*, Fred Standley and Nancy V. Burt, ed. Pp. 94–111. © 1988 by G.K. Hall. Originally published in the *Journal of American Studies* 14, no. 2 (1980): 325–342. Reprinted by permission of The Gale Group.

polemical essay, *The Fire Next Time*, appearing at a crucial moment in black/white relations. Outflanked by the events of the late sixties; he retreated again to Europe. His more recent novels have failed to spark the popular or critical interest of his earlier work.

What follows is not offered as a detailed critical analysis of his literary work but as an account of a career and a mind instructively divided, a sensibility drawn in opposing directions.

James Baldwin spent the first part of his career compensating for his deprivation and the second part compensating for his success. He sought invisibility in racial terms by going to Paris, and ended up by becoming the most visible black writer of his generation. His career was in part generated by the rise of the Civil Rights movement, as white America looked for an explanation for the crisis which had apparently arrived so suddenly; and it was eventually threatened by that movement, which in time produced demands for racial and aesthetic orthodoxy which potentially left him stranded in his equivocal role as mediator and prophet, when the dominant model for black art became fierce commitment and cultural separatism. Having fled a role as writer and individual which was determined by the colour of his skin, he discovered that that colour was in fact to be the key to his art. Wishing to dispense early with the obligation to act as spokesman, he came to recognize a responsibility to articulate, if not the demands, then the feelings of those whose own frustrations and courage were otherwise expressed in mute suffering or simple action. What Baldwin has become he once travelled four thousand miles not to be.

Both the act of refusal and the ultimate acceptance are characteristic gestures of a writer who has always been drawn in two apparently mutually incompatible directions. It was not simply that his early faith in the moral responsibility of the individual and the possibility of social change was destroyed, though he has said as much: "There was a time in my life not so very long ago that I believed, hoped ... that this country could become what it has always presented as what it wanted to become. But I'm sorry, no matter how this may sound: when Martin was murdered for me that hope ended."[1] It is that from the very beginning the optative mood had been in battle with a sullen determinism, the present tense constantly invaded by the past. Catonian warnings in his work have alternated with expressions of sensual salvation. His has indeed always been a schizophrenic style, as he has in turn presented himself as suffering black and alienated American, social outcast and native son. It is a rhetorical style which at its best captured the cadences of hope and rebellion which characterized the early days of the civil rights movement, and which at its worst degenerated into unashamed posturing of a kind which failed to inspect with genuine moral honesty the realities which he had once exposed with such authority.

For Baldwin, the self is sometimes a series of improvisational gestures and sometimes a moral constant which has only to be exposed to become operative. And there is at the heart of his work, beneath the level of contingent event and social determinant, an unexamined confidence in the possibility of action and the recovery of ethical purpose. Constraints are arbitrary and irrational; hatred and rage the product of a history which is real but susceptible of transcendence. Though assailed from within and without by a corrosive mythology, the individual consciousness contains resources entirely adequate to the task of distilling meaning from social chaos, while the alliance of consciousness provides the principal means of resisting an isolation which is part social and part metaphysical.

At the heart of his work is a Christian belief that grace is a gift of suffering and that love has the power to annihilate the primal space between the self and its perception of itself, between the individual and the group. Racial and national categories, though real and though reflecting a symbolic heritage, exist to be transcended, for he is convinced that society clings so desperately to rigid definitions—sexual and social—more from a need to project a sense of order than from, a belief that such distinctions contain any real clue to the nature of human possibilities. The Negro, in fact, is in large part a fiction, a convenient hierarchical invention. As an emblem of unrepressed needs and of uninhibited sexuality, he becomes a convenient image of the dark, spontaneous and anarchic dimension of human life. His social subordination thus stands as a symbol of society's control over its own anarchic impulses. As a consequence he is offered a role whose significance is not limited to its social utility. Thus, when he resists that caricature the consequent appeals by the dominant society to "law and order" have metaphysical as well as pragmatic implications.

In Baldwin's work the self resists the peripheral role which seems its social fate, and the primary agent in this resistance is the imagination. It is an imagination with the necessary power to project alternative worlds, to conceive of a society which can escape its own myths and consciously break its own taboos. The communicative act involved in art (virtually all of his protagonists are artists of one kind or another, including musicians, actors and novelists) becomes in itself a paradigm of a desired social interaction, while the individual's imposition of order, implied by the creative act, becomes a model for a coherence which is generated by the sensibility and not imposed by social fiat. And this presumption of an imaginative control of the world necessarily implies a rejection of that religion which historically has proved a secondary means of social control. Rejection of God is a natural extension of rebellion against the power of the state.

There is a demonstrable logic of revolt. The creation of an autonomous self relies first on a rejection of the authority of the father (his personal revolt against his father recurs in his work) and then that of white society and of God. The self emerges, in a familiar liberal way, by a slow rejection of elements extraneous to that self. Such a process frequently involves pain and Baldwin remains enough of a puritan to believe that this is a key to truth. But salvation, paradoxically, lies in a leap from belief into scepticism. Baldwin places the authority of social and "metaphysical dictat with an authority of the sensibility. Faith gives way to a secular belief in the authenticating power of the self.

Baldwin's characters are highly self-conscious, reflecting not only upon their social situation but on the nature of their consciousness itself. The question of identity is constantly presented to them. Indeed, it is often a clue to literal survival, so that it becomes in itself a literary event. And the particular problem which confronts them is that the usual stratagems of definition now fail. History, memory and belief are at odds with the drive for self-creation and the need for personal alliances which can deny the reality of boundaries. Thus his characters tend to adopt an ambiguous stance with regard to time, appropriating to themselves the right to define process and resist versions of historical progress which threaten to subordinate them to an alien logic.

His use of the internal monologue itself implies the existence of a resistant self which is apart from and not contained by the externalities which otherwise seem to define the limits of action and character. This is the functioning imagination, the artist within, which creates even as it analyses. His are not novels which are primarily concerned with social change in the sense of a re-allocation of power; what matters to him is the altered consciousness of the individual. He is interested in process, in the interplay between the experiential and the given. The stream of consciousness becomes an image for the flow of experience and responses which provide the basis for a definition of the self. And, indeed, in a sense, one can find in William James's discussion of the stream of consciousness a justification for Baldwin's attempt to have his cake and eat it; his feeling that the self is both its own creation and an existent fact which has merely to be exposed to another level of consciousness. In *The Principles of Psychology* William James says that, "if the stream as a whole is identified with the self far more than any outward thing, a *certain portion of the stream abstracted from the rest* is so identified in an altogether peculiar degree, and is felt by all men as a sort of innermost centre within the circle, of sanctuary within the citadel constituted by the subjective life as a whole."[2] For Baldwin this is less a spiritual essence than a sense of moral certainty, an intimate reality available to the individual who learns the necessity to engage experience with a sensibility undistorted by social presumptions.

The problem which Baldwin fails to engage is precisely how that integrity of the self can be projected into a social scale; why the withdrawal into love should be seen as an adequate model for social action since it is frequently born out of a denial of that social action. This is something which he largely leaves to his essays. Baldwin can dramatize the moment and even the process which results in that moment; but he is, for the most part, unable to sustain that moment to the point at which it becomes an enabling strategy. The impersonal power which limits individuality seems too immune to such epiphanies to grant anything but momentary release from its definitional authority.

For Norman Mailer, the world can be made over by the personality, which can counterpose its own energies to that of society and which can release a neutralizing flood of language which, in effect, reduces the physical world to the status of backdrop: the subject of the drama is the self, the social world existing only in so far as the individual is prepared to grant it a role. Personal history becomes as authentic as public history. But for Baldwin history cannot be shrugged off with such a casual gesture. His lack of social freedom, as a Negro, contrasts markedly with that of a man who can seriously run for the office of Mayor of New York, and who apparently has a kind of romantic faith in the fact that social forms are plastic enough to be moulded by the sheer power of the will. As Baldwin has never tired of telling people, the black American knows otherwise. He is all too aware of the injunctions, written and unwritten, which spell out the limits of his freedom; to cross those boundaries is to risk a reaction which is real in the sense of Dr. Johnson's definition of the term. Yet in fact he himself was tempted by solutions every bit as romantic as those advanced by Mailer, and his commitment to invoking the sinister lessons of history is always balanced by a contrary faith in a grace which can dissolve such determinism.

In his attack on Baldwin, in *Advertisements for Myself*, Mailer accused him of not being able to say "Fuck you" to the reader. It was an even more naive remark than it seemed in that it failed to recognize that sense of oppression from which Mailer was immune but which had led Baldwin to be a writer; it also failed to recognize that all of his work was in effect an attempt to discover a basis on which such a contemptuous dismissal of society could be affectuated, while longing, as LeRoi Jones and Eldridge Cleaver cruelly pointed out, for precisely that gesture of inclusion which would obviate such a response.

For Baldwin, will, crucially allied with imagination and a sensitivity to the pressure of other selves, becomes a force with the power, if not to overcome social realities, then to forge other alliances than those sanctioned by history and power. But this is not quite the confident self of the transcendentalists. In each of his books self-analysis is not only provoked by pain; it is the source of pain. Society's power is scarcely diminished. The most that the individual can hope for is to win a small psychic territory within which the harsh pragmatics of the public world no longer operate. Nor is love quite the panacea which it appears, for it, too, is infected by materialism, by the urge to power and by the demands of history and myth. And though, as suggested above, Baldwin is never clear as to whether identity is laboriously constructed out of the interplay of sensibility and event, or whether it is a resilient moral principle concealed beneath social habiliments, in neither sense is he confident of its ability to command public acquiescence. (And this, of course, is the source of the pressure which led him to social protest outside of his novels. As a public spokesman he sought to provoke changes which would allow greater space for the self which, as a novelist, he felt was the real agent of transformation.)

Like Emerson and Thoreau he felt the need to resist those conventions and beliefs which passed for an adequate description of the real, in favour of a spiritual self-reliance, limited only by its obligations to remake the public world, whose deceptions and inadequacies were rejected not in the name of privatism but of truth. But Baldwin inhabits a more sceptical world and his racial identity is forced to concede more power to social fictions than was that of the New England moralist.

In a sense, of course, America has always prided itself on its improvisational qualities, and in his essays Baldwin has repeatedly insisted on the parallel between the Negro in search of selfhood and the American intent of distilling a national identity. And he was clearly right in insisting on his American-ness. It is stamped on his imaginative enterprise. But the fluidities of the American system have historically not extended to the Negro. On this the country had been absolute. Where everything else has changed, to Baldwin this at least has remained a constant. And in this respect the experience of black and white is dissimilar. Certainly the irony of Baldwin claiming an American heritage in his early books of essays at the moment when facilities in southern towns, which he himself was not to visit until his early thirties, were still segregated, was not lost on his critics. Yet Baldwin's view was that though American identity and history had indeed been built on a denial of human complexity and freedom, this was a denial of an essential American idealism to which he wished to lay claim. His resistance to protest fiction (see "Everybody's Protest Novel") and, implicitly, to the naturalistic novel, lay precisely in the fact that it denied access to this idealism, that it made the self into a simple product of biological and environmental determinism. It denied the possibility of escape. And that, arguably, is at the heart of Baldwin's work: the need to forge a truce with determinism and with punishing social constraints, a truce which can sustain the individual even, perhaps, in face of the knowledge of its inevitable collapse. The escape to Europe is simply an attempt to create geographically that space for manoeuvre which in America has to be won through an exertion of imagination or will.

But the ironies emanating from his American identity were not simply those contained in the obvious dissonance between American idealism and reality. As he himself fully realized, his very articulateness is itself fraught with ambiguities which seem to nail him permanently to a paradoxical view of self and cultural identity. Indeed, Baldwin has always been aware of the special problem of language for the black writer. "It is quite possible to say that the price a Negro pays for becoming articulate is to find himself, at length, with nothing to be articulate about."[3] The word becomes a barrier, indeed a protection, between the self and experience. The reduction of social events to language becomes in itself a form of escape. Initially, experience intervenes between the self and the articulation of that experience, but in turn language intervenes between the self and the experience. He is crushed from two directions.

"The root function of language," Baldwin suggests, "is to control the universe by describing it."[4] But the black finds that access to language is not access to power, to control over his environment or himself. Language becomes dysfunctional. Historically, of course, it betrayed him more fully into the power of those who sought to control him by offering means to facilitate that control. And once a possession of that language he becomes, perforce, heir to those very cultural presumptions to which he is formally denied free access. In turn he is then blessed or fated with a fluency which draws him steadily away from his own past. He is thus left with a cultural inheritance characterized by ambiguity, self-doubt, and linguistic paradox. And Baldwin's work carries his mark. The personal pronoun, as he applies it, in *Nobody Knows My Name* and *Notes of a Native Son*, means sometimes Negro and sometimes American, a pronominal uncertainty which goes to the heart of that concern with identity which characterizes so many of his essays and so much of his work. And when he assumes an identification with his American self against his racial identity the effect is more ambivalent. For the cultural nationalists of the sixties his assertion that "Our dehumanization of the Negro ... is indivisible from our dehumanization of ourselves: the loss of our identity is the price we pay for our annulment of his,"[5] is an expression of a desire for cultural assimilation which goes beyond a rhetorical device.

His rhetorical style, particularly that of the latter part of his career, is, in fact a product of the battle to enforce his authority over language, to make it accommodate itself to an experience which it had been designed to justify and impose. As he put it, "you've simply got to force the language to pay attention to you in order to exist in it."[6] The central problem, as he explained to Margaret Mead in 1970, was "how are we ever going to achieve some kind of to me? Because you and I have been involved for all our lives ... in some effort of translation."[7]

Protest was implied in Baldwin's stance as an essayist. He was indeed a mediator, explaining the Negro to America by translating his experience into American terms, by establishing his own struggle for identity as of a kind with that of the American, anxious to distil meaning from history and experience. Like Ralph Ellison, he is essentially calling for the restoration of American idealism, and sees the route to that as lying through the individual: "An honest examination of the national life proves how far we are from the standard of human freedom with which we began. The recovery of this standard demands of everyone who loves this country a hard look at himself, for the greatest achievements must begin somewhere, and they always begin with the person."[8]

His trip to Paris in 1948 was an American search for personal and national identity in an Old World which could render up an image of the New partly from its own desire to translate promise and threat into concrete form, and partly from its own ability to conceive of an American luminous with a meaning derived from those very contradictions which the American writer frequently found so disabling. In part, of course, it was the old game of discovering the limits of the self by abstracting it from the viscous world of its daily setting; it was an attempt to see what could survive such spiritual surgery—an act of definition by elimination, an attempt to find which conflicts were internal and definitional and which part of a dialectic between the unexamined self and the social projections of that self. For a black American it afforded the only opportunity to venture outside of the myth which defined him, and, in a curious way, protected him, in so far as it offered a self-image requiring only acceptance. Here, as Baldwin knew, he would be judged for himself, or at least in the context of other compulsions than the familiar ones. Yet it was as an American that he found himself responding, as an American that Europeans perceived him. And what he learned was the impossibility of distinguishing a clear line between the self and the culture in which that self develops. Once in Europe he felt as "American as any Texas G.I.," freed from the necessary reflexes which had once concealed his own identity from others and hence, eventually, from himself.

It was a move which sprang from the conviction that neither an unquestioned community of suffering, nor an assumed American homogeneity, offered a real clue to personal meaning. Baldwin wanted to find out "in what way the specialness of [his] experience could be made to connect [him] with other people instead of dividing [him] from them."[9] And that specialness could only be abstracted by re-compulsions shaped partly by history and partly by the pressure of a perverted puritanism and a hermeneutic of suffering and guilt.

"Everybody's Protest Novel" was not so much a necessary assault on a major icon of black literature as it was an expression of his desire to resist the role which he could feel being pressed upon him. To be a Negro writer was to be reduced to a socio-literary category. His subject was not just himself, in the sense that it always is for the writer, it was *himself as Negro*. And his assault on the protest novel was an attempt to create sufficient space for himself to operate, outside of the terms which it seemed his fate to embrace. As he said in the introduction to his early book of essays, *Notes of a Native Son*, "I have not written about being a Negro at such length because I expect that to be my only subject, but only because it was the gate I had to unlock before I could hope to write about anything else."[10] At the beginning of his career, already writing his first novel, he felt the need to establish his own right to be seen outside the terms which seemed to mark the limits prescribed for the black novelist, by white society on the one hand, and by the moral demands of black suffering on the other.

He reacted against the Bigger Thomas of Richard Wright's *Native Son*, he admitted, partly because he seemed to him to represent a possibility which had to be rejected if he was to escape a self destructive rage. In an early story, called "Previous Condition," published in 1948, he displaces this violence into the imagination of his protagonist: "I wanted to kill her, I watched her stupid, wrinkled frightened white face and I wanted to take a club, a hatchet, and bring it down with all my weight, splitting her skull down the middle where she parted her iron-grey hair."[11] But Baldwin is less interested in the literal discharge of hatred than in its power to distort the psyche, to warp personal and private history. It was precisely to escape such a distortion that he fled to Europe, a process which he describes in "This Morning, This Evening, So Soon," published in *Going to Meet the Man*, which remains one of his best stories and one which is crucial to an understanding of his position.

It concerns a black American actor/singer who lives in France with a Swedish woman, Harriet, and their son, and is in part an explanation of the sense of release which expatriation granted to him. For though he concedes a determining power to race, religion and nationality, the story is offered as evidence of the fact that such determinants are deadly if they are not transcended: "everyone's life begins on a level where races, armies, and churches stop."[12] And the gift of expatriation is precisely such a transcendence, for it enables individuals to confront themselves and others outside of the constraining power of myth.

Black men and white women free themselves of a public rage and coercive power which, in America, would have become private compulsions. They are also free of a language which might otherwise throw its own reductive net around them. As the protagonist's sister observes, "Language is experience and language is power."[13] The failure of black Americans, as she sees it, is that they employ a language of power which must be ironic since it is detached from their experience. And yet this, of course, is Baldwin's language too and the story can be seen as a confessional work of some honesty. For the protagonist recognizes that his success has in part been generated by a refusal to be identified too closely with the misery of his people, by associating himself, on the contrary, with those responsible for their suffering. It has also been dependent on his refusal to grant any ambiguity to French social attitudes. France had removed the cataract from his eyes, with respect to America, at the cost of a moral myopia with regard to French attitudes.

A brief return to America reminds him that there his life is a concession offered to him by whites. But a conversation with his French director also reminds him that suffering is not a black prerogative. For he had lost a wife and son in the war and knows the weight of history as well as the black American. The real American sin is presented as an innocence of history, a failure to perceive that the past demands a price from the present. And this is a message which Baldwin himself felt increasingly obliged to underline as his career developed.

For Baldwin, Europe's function was precisely to release him from an identity which was no more than a projection of his racial inheritance. It was not, as LeRoi Jones was later to imply, that he wishes to deny his colour but rather that he recognized the danger implicit in allowing public symbols of oppression or resistance to stand as adequate expressions of the self. As he said in his introduction to *Nobody Knows My Name*,

> In America, the colour of my skin had stood between myself and me; in Europe, that barrier was down. Nothing is more desirable than to be released from an affliction, but nothing is more frightening than to be divested of a crutch. It turned out that the question of who I was was not solved because I had removed myself from the social forces which menaced me—anyway, those forces had become interior, and I had

dragged them across the ocean with me. The question of who I was had at last become a personal question, and the answer was to be found in me.[14]

For it was Baldwin's assumption that the question of colour, crucially important on a moral level, concealed a more fundamental problem, the problem of self. And it is in that sense that he felt most American.

But he negotiates a privileged position for himself by claiming an American identity (while naturally disavowing the guilt for a prejudice which he did not originate and for a history which he played no part in determining), and simultaneously embracing a Negro identity (while declining the cultural temporizing and disabling pathology which he otherwise identifies as the natural inheritance of the black American). Both American and Negro search endlessly for identity. Only Baldwin, in the eye of the storm, realizes that it resides in stillness, in an acceptance, not of injustice nor of public roles, but of the authenticity of the self. His failure lies in his inability to reveal the authenticating process at work. Sexuality is clearly a part of it; in some way, supposedly, it tells the truth that the intellect denies. It offers a vital clue, he feels, both to the American need to dramatize innocence and to the real roots of prejudice. In his essay "Nobody Knows My Name," he coyly hints that desegregation battles have to do with "political power and ... with sex."[15] Now, on an obvious level, he is clearly right. It was certainly never an argument about educational theories. But the link between that observation and the obsessive question of identity is not so clear. Meanwhile his own sexual ambiguity was itself a confusing factor, acceptance for him meaning the difficult task of accepting the real nature of his bisexuality, abandoning illusion for reality.

On the face of it the American problem with regard to sex was somewhat different. It was that sexuality had so often been presented as an absolute, as a metaphor for evil or anarchy, or, alternatively, utopian bliss, that it could not be so easily integrated into a realistic model of society. Its metaphoric weight was simply too great. But for Baldwin acceptance implied precisely that elevation of sex into metaphor, so that in virtually all of his work it stands either as an image of exploitation and abuse, or of an innocence with the power to transform social reality: sex as weapon, sex as redemption. In other words he is never more American than in his symbolic perception of sexuality, and what he presents as a kind of emotional realism is in fact a familiar form of sentimentality. It can be found just as easily in Hemingway, in Tennessee Williams, and in Normal Mailer and is no more sophisticated here, except that Mailer, whom Baldwin actually attacked for his sentimentality, purports to see sex as a dialectical term. Baldwin, in struggling to escape the sexual myths which surround the Negro in America, has simply succumbed to others.

He suggests that Wright placed violence where sex should have been, because he was unable to analyse the real nature of the rage which he perceived; but Baldwin himself endows sex with a brutal physicality which is in effect a simple transposition of social violence. Having claimed in his essays that it is principal, in his novels he presents it as agent, while the ambiguities of sexual contact, in part an expression of self, in part a surrender of self, in part aggression, in part submission, become an enactment of the ambivalence implied in the self's confrontation with society and the tensions of racial relationships. For if in suppressing the Negro, white Americans were in fact "burying ... the unspeakably dark, guilty, erotic past which the Protestant fathers made him bury,"[16] then the release of that erotic self should serve to heal the wound opened up by that denial of the whole man. And Baldwin was by no means alone in this assumption. What he adds in the presumption that the existence of the Negro has facilitated his disruption of identity, that he has collaborated in a myth of black sexual potency. The risk is that in releasing this sexuality in his own work he is in danger of endorsing the metaphoric presumptions of those Protestant fathers or, as bad, generating a false image of reconciliation.

In a graceless essay called "Alas, Poor Richard," following Richard Wright's death, he asserted that "the war in the breast between blackness and whiteness which caused Richard such pain, need not be a war. It is a war which just as it denies both the heights and the depths of our natures, takes, and has taken visibly and invisibly, as many white lives as black ones." For him, Wright was "among the most illustrious victims of this war."[17] Borrowing one of Wright's favourite phrases, he had, he suggested, wandered in a no man's land between black and white. The act of reconciliation simply lay beyond Wright's imagination. But what, then, does Baldwin offer? Only, it appears, the fact that whiteness has lost its power and that blackness will soon do so. Thus the crucial act of reconciliation will take place in the moral sensibility of the Negro. But to be made flesh, however, it must assume a reality beyond that privileged environment. And the only way in which he can dramatize it is in the literal embrace of black and white, a coition which, like that implied, but mercifully not enacted, at the end of Hawthorne's *The House of the Seven Gables*, will produce a moral synthesis. The trouble is that, for Baldwin, history cannot be so easily propitiated by simple images of sexual union.

For Baldwin, society is bound together by fear of our unknown selves. In other words, he offers us a neat reversal of the Lockean model. Men form society not to protect their freedom but to evade it. The notion is a Freudian one, so it is perhaps not surprising that the force he invokes to neutralize this process in his work is sexuality. This becomes the key to a real sense of community. The sentimentality of such a conviction is clear and may account for the real evasions which are to be found at the heart of so much of his own work. For social evil is thus seen as deriving from a desire for order and a fear of "our unknown selves ... which can save us—'from the evil that is in the world.'"[18] Indeed by this logic the victim creates himself by accepting the need for social structure and granting it his acquiescence, when all the time "our humanity is our burden, our life; we need not battle for it; we need only to do what is infinitely more difficult—that is, accept it."[19]

In the case of his attack on *Native Son*, he is offering a severe misreading, for far from being trapped within sociological generalizations, far from reducing complexity to simplicity and failing to engage the dangerous but liberating freedom of the individual, the genuinely subversive quality of that novel lies not in its attack on American society but in its conviction that individual action and the individual mind are not socially determined or socially bound. It is true that Wright's novel was a curiously schizophrenic work, with the individualistic drive of the narrative operating against an adjectival insistence on constriction and the deterministic weight implied by its sectional headings: Fear, Flight, Fate. It is equally true that, if events constitute successive stages in the liberation of the sensibility, they are also, by inverse law, stages in the diminishing world of social possibilities. But Baldwin was saddled with the same paradox. He wishes to presume both that the self is real and pre-social, and that it cannot exist apart from its determinants. The result is a curious and distinctive tension between what he sees as an American sensibility and a free-ranging existential self—yet another example of his manichean imagination which sees himself as the product of the Old World and the

New, black and white, vengeance and love, male and female; probing intellect and liberating imagination. It is a dialectical process of which the self is the putative synthesis. And, to Baldwin, this is an American process.

To Baldwin, the objective of the novelist is to serve truth, which he defines as "a devotion to the human being, his freedom and fulfilment." To see the individual as only an image of a race is to exchange reality for symbol, a life for a cause. And this was the real target of "Everybody's Protest Novel"—the retreat into metaphor. And just as Moby Dick was not to be understood either as type or as emblem, so the individual's reality lies outside his availability as public symbol. Baldwin could already feel the pressure of the public role he was inevitably offered and which he felt the need to resist. "What is today offered as his [the black writer's] Responsibility," he said, "is, when he believes it, his corruption and our loss."[20] Curiously, Native Son's vulnerability to Baldwin's criticism lay less in the element of protest, which is the source of its central ambiguity, than in the vague mythologizing of the social impulse which Bigger Thomas feels. The edge of his newly-discovered identity blurs at the very moment of its, coalescence. Baldwin suggests that American uncertainty about identity, and American disregard for the identity of others, derive from a contempt for history and historical process. Doubtful of historical logic, the American has tended to distrust time and to value experience—to assume that identity therefore is the product of events outside of time. A name is no more than the emblem of a man until it is claimed in action. The result is a social formlessness which masquerades as freedom but actually smacks of anarchy. And this breeds a Hemingwayesque pragmatic morality which is as likely to validate racism as anything else. It is, he suggests, an American confusion to think that it is possible to consider the person apart from all the forces which have produced him, since American history turns on the abstraction of the individual from his social and cultural setting. And yet this is precisely Baldwin's assumption, since, as we have seen above, when it serves his purpose he too posits the existence of a primary self outside of and unaffected by history. This, indeed, is a clue to a basic contradiction in his position which enables him both to use the moral self to indict the social world and the social world to explain the collapse of self.

The recurring pain to which Baldwin avers in the alienation from self and from the cultural experience of the Negro, an alienation which is not neutralized by expatriation, as this intensifies the guilt and adds a further level of ambiguity since now he must battle for possession of an American identity which if the source of his pain, is also the key to its transcendence. As he puts it in a 1950 essay, "Encounter on the Seine," "To accept the reality of his being an American becomes a matter involving his integrity and his greatest hopes, for only by accepting this reality can he hope to make articulate to himself or to others the uniqueness of his experience, and to set free the spirit so long anonymous and caged."[21] More than this, like Wright, he felt that the black experience not merely offered a clue to American moral ambiguity but that it functioned as metaphor, that "in white Americans he finds reflected—repeated, as it were, in a higher key—his tensions, his terrors, his tenderness" and that "in this need to establish himself in relation to his past he is most American, that this depthless alienation from oneself and one's people is, in sum, the American experience."[22]

Having previously argued, in his essay on the protest novel, against metaphoric reductivism, he now strains, as expatriate, to transform his own experience into an emblem of dispossession in precisely the same way that Wright had done in a series of works starting with *Native Son* and running through "The Man Who Lived Underground" and *The Outsider*. Where he does try to establish a distinction it is that between the social and the metaphysical image, yet this is a distinction which he finds it difficult to sustain. It now turns out that his real rejection of Wright's novel lies in what he takes to be the inaccuracy of its portrait, in its faulty sociology, a conviction that the problem is being engaged too soon, at a level which denies not so much the complexity of the Negro as that of an essential human nature. For he feels that "the battle is elsewhere. It proceeds far from us in the heat and horror and pain of life itself where all men are betrayed by greed and guilt and blood lust and where no man's hands are clean."[23] It remains unexamined since, as Camus realized, the logic of this position is that if all men are guilty then all men are innocent. If the sociological approach implies the possibility of facile solutions then assertions of an immutable human nature, generating social action, leave one with the sentimentalities of evil and innocence, with desperate images such as that which concludes but scarcely resolves Steinbeck's *The Grapes of Wrath*, in which social realities are invited to defer before the reassertion of human goodness. For this was a paradox he was not ready to engage, indeed has never engaged, since he has continued to dramatize human action as a battle between good and evil, a battle which he believes to characterize American political and cultural presumptions. Out of the sociological frying pan and into the metaphysical fire. Knowing that "anyone who insists on remaining in a state of innocence long after that innocence is dead, turns himself into a monster,"[24] his puritan mentality continued to play with manichean ideas.

The essence of his contradictions was exposed very effectively in a conversation between Baldwin and Margaret Mead which took place in 1970—a discussion in which the anthropologist acts as a useful restraining influence on the writer's sentimentalities and on his increasingly casual use of language. Baldwin was intent on establishing an historical guilt, incurred by the act of enslavement, but inherited by white Americans of the present. In this respect, he admitted himself to be something of an Old Testament prophet. But he also wished to offer the possibility of absolution, and the resultant contradiction between an ineradicable guilt and a necessary grace, which has characterized so much of his work, was carefully exposed by Margaret Mead. Speaking of the process of enslavement of blacks, he describes it as "the crime which is spoken of in the Bible, the sin against the Holy Ghost which cannot be forgiven."[25] The exchange which followed reveals his tendency to let language and imagery outstrip his convictions:

MEAD:	Then we've nowhere to go.
BALDWIN:	No, we have atonement.
MEAD:	Not for the sin against the Holy Ghost.
BALDWIN:	No?
MEAD:	I mean, after all, you were once a theologian.... And the point about the sin against the Holy Ghost is that—
BALDWIN:	Is that it cannot be forgiven.
MEAD:	So if you state a crime as impossible of forgiveness you've doomed everyone.
BALDWIN:	No. I don't think I was as merciless as the Old Testament prophets. But I do agree with Malcolm X, that sin demands atonement.
MEAD:	Whose sin? I mean, you're making racial guilt.
BALDWIN:	No.

MEAD:	Yes. You are.
BALDWIN:	I'm not talking about race. I'm talking about the fact.
MEAD:	But you are.... You're taking an Old Testament position, that the sins of the fathers are visited on their children.
BALDWIN:	They are.
MEAD:	The consequences are visited on the children.
BALDWIN:	It's the same thing, isn't it?
MEAD:	No, it's not the same thing at all. Because it's one thing to say, All right, I'm suffering for what my fathers did—
BALDWIN:	I don't mean that, I don't mean that! I don't mean that at all! I mean something else! I mean something which I may not be able to get to ...
MEAD:	... but when you talk about atonement you're talking about people who weren't *born* when this was committed.
BALDWIN:	No. I mean the recognition of where one finds oneself in time or history or now.... After all, I'm not guiltless, either. I sold my brothers or my sisters—
MEAD:	When did you?
BALDWIN:	Oh, a thousand years ago, it doesn't make any difference.
MEAD:	It *does* make a difference. I think if one takes that position it's absolutely hopeless. I will *not* accept any guilt for what anybody else did. I will accept guilt for what I did myself.[26]

Jean-Paul Sartre makes a similar point in *Anti-Semite and Jew* when he observes that "if one is going to reproach little children for the sins of their grandfathers, one must first of all have a very primitive conception of what constitutes responsibility."[27]

What Baldwin's comments to Margaret Mead demonstrate is a desire, evident throughout his published works, to present history as present reality, to establish a social responsibility which, because he chooses to dramatize it in terms of sin and guilt, he is unable to establish as an active principle. The Old Testament prophet denies the efficacy of New Testament grace. The writer who wishes to establish a racial indictment is thus inhibited from dramatizing the need for racial reconciliation which is a conviction which he holds with equal force. His desire to establish his belief that individuals are responsible moral creatures is simultaneously undermined by his conviction that their crime is ineradicable and human beings ineluctably wicked. The problem does not reside in language alone, but in his own terrible ambivalences which lead him to accuse and defend, condemn and rescue with equal conviction. The deficiency is an intellectual one.

Even now, in one mood, he sees a solution in some kind of symbolic union of black and white for which he can find no historic justification and for which he can establish no social mechanism. When asked, some twenty-five years after his first essay, how he meant to go about securing his solution to the problem, his reply was simply "I don't know yet." And then, slipping into the opposite mood, which has always been the other side to this sentimental vision, he offered the only solution which he could see: "Blow it up."[28]

Notes

1. James Baldwin and Margaret Mead, *A Rap on Race* (London: 1972), pp. 245–46.

2. Quoted in Frederick Hoffman, *The Mortal No* (Princeton: 1964), p. 332.

3. James Baldwin, *Notes of a Native Son* (London: 1965), p. 3.

4. Ibid., p. 141.

5. Ibid., p. 19.

6. Baldwin and Mead, *A Rap on Race*, p. 58.

7. Ibid., p. 180.

8. James Baldwin, *Nobody Knows My Name* (London: 1965), p. 98.

9. Ibid., p. 17.

10. Baldwin, *Notes of a Native Son*, p. 5.

11. James Baldwin, *Going to Meet the Man* (New York: 1966), p. 76.

12. Ibid., p. 127.

13. Ibid., p. 129.

14. Baldwin, *Nobody Knows My Name*, p. 11.

15. Ibid., p. 87.

16. Ibid., p. 169.

17. Ibid.

18. Baldwin, *Notes of a Native Son*, p. 15.

19. Ibid., p. 17.

20. Ibid., p. 11.

21. Ibid., p. 102.

22. Ibid., p. 104.

23. Ibid., p. 35.

24. Ibid., p. 148.

25. James Baldwin and Margaret Mead, *A Rap on Race* (London: 1972), p. 18.6.

26. Ibid., pp. 186–87.

27. Jean-Paul Sartre, *Anti-Semite and Jew*, trans. G.J. Becker (New York: 1965), 16.

28. Baldwin and Mead, *A Rap on Race*, p. 250.

Chronology

1924	James Arthur Baldwin born on August 2 in Harlem, New York, to Emma Berdis Jones.
1927	Emma Berdis Jones marries David Baldwin.
1930–38	Attends P.S. 24 and Frederick Douglass Junior High School where he studies with poet Countee Cullen.
1938	Becomes a Young Minister at the Fireside Pentecostal Assembly in Harlem.
1942	Graduates from De Witt Clinton High School; renounces the ministry.
1943	David Baldwin dies on July 29.
1944	Moves to Greenwich Village.
1945	Baldwin meets novelist Richard Wright; receives Eugene Saxton Fellowship.
1947	First professional publication, the review "Maxim Gorky as Artist," appears in the *Nation* magazine.
1948	Receives Rosenwald Fellowship; Baldwin leaves for Paris, France, on November 11.
1949	Meets Lucien Happersberger.
1953	*Go Tell It on the Mountain* published to critical praise.
1954	Completes first play, *The Amen Corner*; receives a Guggenheim.
1955	Baldwin's first book of nonfiction, *Notes of a Native Son*, published.

1956	*Giovanni's Room*, groundbreaking novel about homosexuality, published; receives the National Institute of Arts & Letters Award.
1957	Visits the American South for the first time; writes first essays on the civil rights movement for *Harper's* and *Partisan Review*.
1959	Ford Foundation Grant.
1961	Second collection of essays, *Nobody Knows My Name*, published.
1962	*Another Country*, best-selling novel, published; Baldwin travels to Africa; meets the Honorable Elijah Muhammad of the Nation of Islam in Chicago.
1963	*The Fire Next Time* published; Baldwin awarded the George Polk Memorial Award for magazine reporting; meets with U.S. attorney general Robert F. Kennedy.
1964	*Blues for Mister Charlie* opens on Broadway; *Nothing Personal* published; Baldwin elected to the National Institute of Arts and Letters.
1965	*The Amen Corner* produced on Broadway; *Going to Meet the Man*, a collection of short stories, published.
1968	Publication of the novel *Tell Me How Long the Train's Been Gone* and the play *The Amen Corner* opens on Broadway.
1971	*A Rap on Race*, with anthropologist Margaret Mead, published.
1972	*No Name in the Street*, an essay on the Civil Rights Movement, and *One Day, When I Was Lost*, an unproduced screenplay about the life of Malcolm X, published.
1973	Publication of *A Dialogue* with the poet and activist, Nikki Giovanni.
1974	Publication of fifth novel, *If Beale Street Could Talk*.
1976	Awarded honorary doctorate from Morehouse College; publishes *The Devil Finds Work*.
1979	Publication of last novel, *Just Above My Head*.
1982	Awarded honorary doctorate from the City University of New York.

1985   Publication of *The Price of the Ticket: Collected Nonfiction, 1948–1985.*

1986   Awarded the Commander of the Legion d'Honneur by France's president, François Mitterrand.

1987   Dies on December 1 in St. Paul-de-Vence; funeral on December 8 at the Cathedral of St. John the Divine in New York City.

Works by James Baldwin

Go Tell It on the Mountain, 1953.

Notes of a Native Son, 1955.

Giovanni's Room, 1956.

Nobody Knows My Name, 1961.

Another Country, 1962.

The Fire Next Time, 1963.

Nothing Personal, with photographs by Richard Avedon, 1964.

Blues for Mister Charlie, 1964.

Going to Meet the Man, 1965.

Tell Me How Long the Train's Been Gone, 1968.

The Amen Corner, 1968.

A Rap on Race, with Margaret Mead, 1971.

One Day, When I Was Lost, 1972.

No Name in the Street, 1972.

A Dialogue, with Nikki Giovanni, 1973.

If Beale Street Could Talk, 1974.

Little Man, Little Man: A Story of Childhood, 1976.

The Devil Finds Work, 1976.

Just Above My Head, 1979.

Jimmy's Blues: Selected Poems, 1983.

The Evidence of Things Not Seen, 1985.
The Price of the Ticket: Collected Nonfiction, 1948–1985, 1985.

Works about James Baldwin

Balfour, Katharine Lawrence. *The Evidence of Things Not Said: James Baldwin and the Promise of American Democracy*. Ithaca, New York: Cornell University Press, 2001.

Bloom, Harold, ed. *Modern Critical View: James Baldwin*. New York: Chelsea House, 1986.

Burt, Nancy V. and Fred L. Standley, ed. *Critical Essays on James Baldwin*. Boston: G.K. Hall, 1988.

Campbell, James. *Talking at the Gates: A Life of James Baldwin*. New York: Penguin Books, 1991.

———. *Exiled in Paris: Richard Wright, James Baldwin, Samuel Beckett, and Others on the Left Bank*. New York: Scribner, 1995.

Clark, Keith. *Black Manhood in James Baldwin, Ernest J. Gaines, and August Wilson*. Urbana: University of Illinois Press, 2002.

de Romanet, Jerome. "Revisiting Madeleine and *The Outing*: James Baldwin's Revision of Gide's Sexual Politics." *Melus* 22.1 (Spring 1997): 3–15.

Eckman, Fern M. *The Furious Passage of James Baldwin*. New York: M. Evans, 1966.

Gottfried, Ted *James Baldwin: Voice From Harlem*. New York: F. Watts, 1997.

Harris, Trudier. *Black Women in the Fiction of James Baldwin*. Knoxville: University of Tennessee Press, 1985.

Kinnamon, Keneth. *James Baldwin: A Collection of Critical Essays.* Englewood Cliffs, N.J.: Prentice-Hall, 1974.

Leeming, David A. *James Baldwin: A Biography.* New York: Knopf, 1994.

Macebuh, Stanley. *James Baldwin: A Critical Study.* NewYork: Third Press, 1973.

McBride, Dwight A, ed. *James Baldwin Now.* New York: New York University Press, 1999.

Miller, D. Quentin, ed. *Re-Viewing James Baldwin: Things Not Seen.* Philadelphia: Temple University Press, 2000.

O'Daniel, Therman B. *James Baldwin: A Critical Evaluation.* Washington: Howard University Press, 1977.

Ohi, Kevin. "'I'm Not the Boy You Want': Sexuality, 'Race,' and Thwarted Revelation in Baldwin's *Another Country.*" *African American Review* 33.2 (Summer 1999): 261–83.

Olson, Barbara K. "'Come-to-Jesus-Stuff' in James Baldwin's *Go Tell It on the Mountain* and *The Amen Corner.*" *African American Review* 31.2 (Summer 1997): 295.

Porter, Horace. *Stealing the Fire The Art and Protest of James Baldwin.* Middletown, Conn: Wesleyan University Press, 1989.

Pratt, Louis H. *James Baldwin.* Boston: G.K. Hall and Co., 1978.

Rosset, Lisa. *James Baldwin.* New York: Chelsea House Publishers, 1989.

Scott, Lynn Orilla. *James Baldwin's Later Fiction: Witness to the Journey.* East Lansing: Michigan State University Press, 2002.

Standley, Fred, and Louis H. Pratt. ed. *Conversations with James Baldwin.* Jackson: University Press of Mississippi, 1989.

Tóibín, Colm. *Love in a Dark Time.* London: Picador, 2002.

Troup, Quincy, ed., *James Baldwin: The Legacy.* New York: Simon & Schuster, 1989.

Weatherby, W.J. *James Baldwin: An Artist on Fire.* New York: Donald I. Fine Inc, 1990.

Websites

Today in Literature: James Baldwin
www.todayinliterature.com/biography/james.baldwin.asp#stories

More on James Baldwin: from the Archives of the *New York Times*
http://partners.nytimes.com/books/98/03/29/specials/baldwin.html

PBS—American Masters
www.pbs.org/wnet/americanmasters/database/baldwin_j.html

Contributors

HAROLD BLOOM is Sterling Professor of the Humanities at Yale University. He is the author of over 20 books, including *Shelley's Mythmaking* (1959), *The Visionary Company* (1961), *Blake's Apocalypse* (1963), *Yeats* (1970), *A Map of Misreading* (1975), *Kabbalah and Criticism* (1975), *Agon: Toward a Theory of Revisionism* (1982), *The American Religion* (1992), *The Western Canon* (1994), and *Omens of Millennium: The Gnosis of Angels, Dreams, and Resurrection* (1996). *The Anxiety of Influence* (1973) sets forth Professor Bloom's provocative theory of the literary relationships between the great writers and their predecessors. His most recent books include *Shakespeare: The Invention of the Human* (1998), a 1998 National Book Award finalist, *How to Read and Why* (2000), *Genius: A Mosaic of One Hundred Exemplary Creative Minds* (2002), *Hamlet: Poem Unlimited* (2003), and *Where Shall Wisdom be Found* (2004). In 1999, Professor Bloom received the prestigious American Academy of Arts and Letters Gold Medal for Criticism, and in 2002 he received the Catalonia International Prize.

AMY SICKELS is a freelance writer living in New York City. She received her MFA in creative writing from Penn State University and she has published short stories, essays, and book reviews in numerous journals, including *Fourth Genre*, *Kalliope*, and *Literary Review*.

GABRIEL WELSCH's short stories, poems, and reviews have appeared in *Georgia Review*, *Mid-American Review*, *Crab Orchard Review*, and

Cream City Review. He regularly reviews literature for *Harvard Review*, *Missouri Review*, *Slope*, and *Small Press Review*. He received a Pennsylvania Council on the Arts Fellowship for Literature in fiction in 2003.

LYNN ORILLA SCOTT is a Visiting Assistant Professor in the Department of American Thought and Language at Michigan State University. *James Baldwin's Later Fiction: Witness to the Journey* (2002) is her first widely circulated publication.

C.W.E. BIGSBY is a professor of American Studies at the University of East Anglia. He has published more than thirty books on theatre and literature. His publications include *Modern American Drama* (2000) and *Arthur Miller: A Critical Study* (2004).

Index

Characters in literary works are indexed by first name (if any), followed by the name of the work in parentheses.